IT STARTED
WITH A PAIL

T0147970

IT STARTED WITH A PAIL

DON LITCHKO

iUniverse, Inc.
Bloomington

IT STARTED WITH A PAIL

Copyright © 2013 by Don Litchko.

All rights reserved. No part of this book may be used or reproduced by any means, graphic, electronic, or mechanical, including photocopying, recording, taping or by any information storage retrieval system without the written permission of the publisher except in the case of brief quotations embodied in critical articles and reviews.

iUniverse books may be ordered through booksellers or by contacting:

iUniverse
1663 Liberty Drive
Bloomington, IN 47403
www.iuniverse.com
1-800-Authors (1-800-288-4677)

Because of the dynamic nature of the Internet, any web addresses or links contained in this book may have changed since publication and may no longer be valid. The views expressed in this work are solely those of the author and do not necessarily reflect the views of the publisher, and the publisher hereby disclaims any responsibility for them.

Any people depicted in stock imagery provided by Thinkstock are models, and such images are being used for illustrative purposes only.
Certain stock imagery © Thinkstock.

ISBN: 978-1-4759-6936-8 (sc)
ISBN: 978-1-4759-6937-5 (ebk)

Printed in the United States of America

iUniverse rev. date: 1/07/2013

Acknowledgements

Three women deserve special recognition for any pleasures derived from this group of stories.

First and foremost my wife, Carole Ann, who graciously tolerated my taking a few hours each week to write for pleasure; and occasionally pirate funds from the family budget for ink, paper, stamps and other materials; all so that I could send out the weekly Litchko Newsletter; this she has tolerated for nearly twenty five years without ever a complaint. For nearly forty five years she has been my most consistent source of support and encouragement.

Second, my Mom, who besides bringing me into this world has always encouraged each of her children to "reach out and go for it;" and then somehow managed to find time for prayers when one of us reached out a little further than she had anticipated. I suspect she has spent more time praying for me than for my brothers or sister.

Third for a woman that I knew for much too short a time, Jewel Farrar; she was an English teacher and the mother of Marlowe; one of my best friends. I'm certain that if she were still alive that the punctuation and grammatical errors you will find in my paragraphs would have all been eliminated; her command of the language would have been a great side benefit. Jewels biggest gift, the one she did share during our time together, came by way of example. Jewel loved life; be it the trail an ant might leave in the dirt, or how to navigate by the stars, or understanding how the court systems worked so that she could be a child advocate, or learning how to handle sled dogs. Her interests were even more varied than mine;, and she was the perfect example of how one should enjoy and be a part of life long after others start thinking that 'I'm too old for that." Jewel just never took the time to grow old.

Many others have influenced my life, but these three are special and I love them each.

Preface

This book is a collection of stories written over the past twenty five years from what has become known as the Litchko Newsletters.

I am a native of Kirkwood and Windsor, New York; neighboring towns east of Binghamton. I think the town line went right through my parent's home or very close; I often told people that I slept in Windsor but ate breakfast in Kirkwood. Thanks to good planning on my Mom and Dad's part I was able to grow up on a hundred wooded acres a couple miles off of Route 11, on Trim Street.

For nearly twenty-five years I worked in Aerospace before accepting a position in Arlington, Texas. Three of our four children were in college and Texas tuitions were most acceptable compared to colleges in the Northeast.

But alas, like for all, life played some tricks and we found ourselves relocating back east to New Hampshire, sadly leaving our three oldest in Texas. I missed them something fierce. So each Sunday morning before going to Mass I would sit down and write them a letter; supposedly a newsletter; but in truth there was only so much family news each week so I started to include old family stories, occasionally a little fiction; occasionally some fiction comingled with facts; more often than not trying to bring a few smiles to the reader. Our correspondence was by E Mail.

The kids started sending my rantings to cousins and friends with comments like, "Wait till you read what the old man wrote this week," and soon a distribution list was started that eventually grew to over six hundred readers each week.

Then one day I got some family hate mail. "I use to kiss your little feet and wipe your bottom, but I'm not good enough to get a letter like everyone else." Mom did not, and does not, have a computer, but starting then and to this day she gets a snail mail copy every week.

The stories are not complied in any particular order; because that is not how grandpas tell stories; we just share whatever comes to mind when it happens to come to mind; and there are days when we are darn thankful anything comes to mind.

Read each and enjoy. Should it bring back a good memory, great. Should it make you smile, that is what was intended; and should just one of you read and break out in a good old fashion giggle I will considered myself a success.

Love you all

From a Hill Far Away

In Conway, New Hampshire

Where sometimes even the owls don't give a hoot.

Remembrance

My earliest unaided recollection is of a farmhouse on Kent Street in Windsor, New York.

Based on photos and stories my parents passed on, my mind sometimes thinks I remember things like a collie dog named Bowzer that thought it was a coon hound and had a reputation for chasing patched eyed bandits by climbing right up the trees; or when my Aunt Evelyn drowned in the Susquehanna River across from the Alice Freeman Palmer school during a school picnic; or how it was when all the guys were hunting deep in the woods on top of the second highest hill in Broome County while Grandpa Urda just stayed in the barn and waited for the big twelve point buck to come out to the apple tree, a hundred feet from the barn, and how he got it with just one shot.

Sometimes I think I remember the look on my mother's face as she looked out the window from my parent's second floor apartment on Ronan Street in Binghamton, and saw me, her toddler, shooting down the hill, alone in my wagon, eyes wide open, hair straight back in the wind; oblivious to the traffic as I shot across the Baxter Street intersection to parts unknown—and how the old Slovak women on the street yelled "Mairo, Mairo" (Mary, Mary) as I went by. As if my mother could have run down a flight of stairs and out to the front of the house in time to catch me. The devil himself could not have caught me that day.

Sometimes I think I remember those things; but I really don't.

The farmhouse sat on a hill off the road near where the Beaver Lake Road intersects with Kent Street. There were three large clumps of lilacs in the front, so thick that the only time you could see the house from the road was in the winter when the leaves were off. There were large single pane glass windows in the front that went nearly from the ceiling to the floor. They were that kind of glass that had little bubbles and manufacturing imperfections; and a little boy could see the flaws and flows that somehow perfected his daydreams. They were that kind that cracked when a little boy leaned heavily against them. The kind of cracking sound that made a round shaped, round faced, pure white haired woman holler "Mairo, Mairo—Yoy Bousa" (Oh God)—"He is going true (through)." It cracked, I didn't, and my mother's hair started to turn as white as her mother's. The window has a long diagonal line through it to this day.

The whole house was great. There were bedrooms with a big brass bed in each. On each bed was a perina (goose down coverlet) all fluffed up that felt like a cloud when my Dad would toss me on it. The perina's were the only things my grandmother was able to bring with her from Czechoslovakia when at eighteen she left her parents and all alone came to America. Grandma had the courage of a soldier, the business wisdom of a Wall Street executive; and faith enough to humble the Pope.

There was a half attic off one of the upstairs bedrooms which was a combination storage room, tool shop, and recreation room inasmuch as it had a four by eight sheet of plywood on a couple of saw horses. There was a net across it and two sandpaper paddles somewhere; and there were lots of places for Ping Pong balls to hide. There were yellow jackets and hornets all over the windows in the summer time—enough to keep a little boy always near the door, just in case. And in the winter it became a big refrigerator where platters of lacvor, poppy seed, apricot and ground walnut kolackies were stored for consumption after Christmas midnight mass. Yep that attic was an important place to a little explorer.

Downstairs on the first floor was a rather formal living room; where nobody ever went; it was the only stuffy place in the house. Closed off in the winter to save heat; it was used to store presents for Saint Nick; and only occasionally used in the summer. The room did have one thing that frequently caught my fancy; an Arabian looking lamp. It had a brass base and an oval brass shade decorated with scribing and perforations. All along the edge of the shade hung strings of amber beads that rattled, tangled and sometime broke when little hands played with them. And every time I got within fifty feet of that lamp someone would holler "Yoy Bosua—Mairooooooo."

The dining room took up most of the front of the house. It had linoleum over most of the floor that got slippery when it was wet and, and slippery-er yet when my Uncles would place me on an old gray wool army blanket and drag and spin me around as a human buffer. It had to be because I can clearly remember years later when the house finally got wired for electricity.

The room had a large, round oak table in the middle that was supported by wooden lions feet. Each chair had the face of a man carved into the back rest that looked like Old Man Wind; and when it was my turn to dust for grandma my fingers would slide down through the smooth gullies that formed the whiskers. In one corner was a black leather couch that had brass decorator nails in patterns around the edges. This is where my Uncle Fred would read his dime store mysteries with the dirty covers; sometimes the pictures showed a girl's leg above the knee. Sometimes I would use the couch as a slide and zip down the arms when Uncle Fred wasn't in it.

There was a Singer sewing machine near the wall by the stairs; one that you had to peddle; the kind that a little boy could explore underneath and take off the round leather cord that went from the trundle to the flywheel—it was the kind that is now a table at some Spaghetti Warehouse. Next to it, in the corner was a large china cabinet with a curved glass door. It sort of matched the table.

On one wall was a large picture of the Sacred Heart of Jesus that grandma would look at every morning when she said her rosary. There was a tall ornate wood burning stove that sat on a tin floor protector where a small boy could make roads with his fingers in the ashes that sometimes dropped there. Behind the stove was a little built in bookshelf type closet with a cloth door where I could hide and listen when the big people talked seriously, in broken English. It was the same little closet where I could cuddle up and take a warm winter nap because one of the walls was actually the chimney for the wood stove.

The best part of the room was the corner by the stairs where there was a built in hutch that had a large window on each side of it. In the hutch was kept blue and indigo glassware with pressed in patterns. When exposed to the morning or evening sun the glass would reflect neat shadows on the floors and walls. Stored in the bottom of the hutch was a little unfinished wooden box that had a different smell; a smell developed over years of use as a butter press. The stairs were where a little guy could climb and get taller than his Uncles and where he could look down on everything. The stairs were special.

The kitchen had a pantry under the stairs where boxes of cereal were kept. It was where my grandmother would let me wiggle my fingers into a box of Mother Oats to find the free dish or cup. It was where you could check out the box of Puffed Rice to see if it had cutout airplanes on the back. Shredded Wheat was in an ammo shaped box and in between the rows were cards with Indian tracking lore on them.

The kitchen had a sink with only cold running water that came through copper pipes down from a spring on the hill. It wasn't a deep well or treated city water. It was water so sweet that the frogs loved to swim in it; and I clearly remember walking up to the spring and watching them do so.

The floors were bare wood; wide planks bleached white from the Clorox my grandmother would put on them every Friday. Floors that went click, click, click when a baby lamb or piglet was brought down from the barn for me to play with. Floors that turned gray when I splashed in the big round tub on bath nights.

There was a table with a big baking board on it; the one my dad had made, which my grandmother would lean into when she kneaded bread dough; the dough she made without a recipe. Grandma would sift a mountain of flour and then make a hole in the top in which she placed eggs, milk, yeast and some salt; it remind me of a volcano. It was the same table where she would roll out egg noodle dough and then slice it so fast with a machete like knife that just slid off her finger tips; such that the men would always hold up her hand and count five whenever she was done to see if her fingers were all there. It was the table where warm bread was put when removed from the pans and then covered with melted butter (applied with a cleaned white chicken feather) to keep the tops soft. The same bread that the men would run all the way from the barn for, just to get the heels—first.

There was a wood burning cooking stove with a warming rack on top. A stove with a surface that flat breads two feet across could be baked on; flat breads with sugar and yellow turmeric on top; or flat breads with fired cabbage inside that were just always there for snacking. It was a wood stove where people would take their boots off and stick their feet in the oven while visiting on cold winter evenings. It was a good stove.

It was in reality a poor hill farm where the owners were so poor that in the beginning they had to carry the manure out to the fields in old bushel baskets.

But it was a good house. A house with values and a work ethic that eventually produced independent business men, a store owner, a county clerk, a bronze star recipient, the contractor who built much of Cape Canaveral, and the woman who washed my bottom and kissed my little feet. That I remember.

Behind the stove was a walk in closet. It too had a heavy drape for a door. This was the closet that smelled of hay, animals and their surroundings, of dirt and sawdust, lime and fertilizer. This closet was dark and had no light. Long and narrow it was lined on both sides by the work clothes of my Uncles and grandfather. At the far end was a white pail with a flared top, and the pail had a cover; when the cover was removed, depending on the time of day, the pail smelled. I never yearned to remove that cover.

It was night. It was cold and why the cow was due to freshen this time of year I didn't know. I didn't even know what the word freshen meant. But Grandpa had to check her out and the first words I can remember were "Donnie—Yoy Bousea." Rather than lift that cover I had pee'd in his boot.

It started with a pail.

◉ ◉ ◉ ◉ ◉

SALLY

In the past seventy years there have been many pails and a lot of covers I still don't want to lift. So the ensuing words will not dwell on sadness, nor ring with bitterness and pout. Instead, they will capture some of the adventures of growing up; a process that has yet to stop. This will not be a biography. I have studied the mall book stores by the hour and have yet to see anyone buying a biography; even when they are on a cart by the door and marked down to $2.95. One does not get rich writing a biography. Nor will this be a book about sex. I am not running for public office so I don't have to tell. Not that I didn't share in some of the adventures of youth like putting mirrors inside my shoe strings and trying to maneuver my fifth grade foot to a position where I could get a peek. And I do remember those fifties locker room jokes about "How can you tell if a girl is wearing panties?" Look for dandruff on her shoes. "How can you tell if a girl is wearing panty hose?' When she breaks wind her ankles swell. And then there was Sally—I met Sally in Phoenix.

To say that Sally was attractive would be an understatement. To say Sally was well endowed would not be an overstatement. To say the Sally was smart would be honest; but most males didn't care. And to say that Sally enjoyed being a sweater girl was an unequivocal fact.

The Quality Control office in which I worked was not yet into PC.s, digital calculators or word processors back in the early sixties. It did have one electric analog calculator that ten or twenty aspiring engineers could share, and use to sum the squares and calculate the area under the curve; determine two or three sigma limits, and all that good stuff.

I had been pounding numbers for a half hour when I felt the presence of someone leaning over me; someone who obviously wanted to use the machine; someone who was annoying me and interrupting my train of thought. At the end of the next string of numbers I swiveled around and immediately found my nose two inches away from Sally's bare navel. The sweater girl was bored waiting and was in the middle of a yawn. Hands up over her head; the sweater had pulled up. I don't know why, maybe I instinctively knew I would never be that close to that navel again and felt I should do something to mark the occasion. Without thinking, faster than Zorro with his sword, I took my ball point pen and made an "X", a BIG "X' right across Sally's bare navel. "X" marked the spot.

She said "Oh"

I said "Ah Ha"

And J.B., behind me said "Ahem" in a tone that did not reek of good will. J.B was not the group leader, the unit manager or even the section manager. No. no, JB was so far up the ladder I don't know how he even found our office. I didn't even think he spoke the same language I did; at least he wasn't mumbling the way I was.

The human mind works faster than a computer and in a split second I thought:

My career is over—I'm dead—He will tell my mother—Maybe she is his daughter or niece or something—How will I put this on my resume—Is there a hole under this table—I did it—I really did it.

Sally, bless her heart, saved the day and my career. She walked over to J.B. pulled up her sweater to expose the "X"; smiled and said "look at that." J.B. couldn't help but look. The rest of the office laughed, loud, and J.B. got very red in the cheeks. He started to mumble and I thought for a second that we might be able to communicate after all. And then he left never to be seen in that office again.

She sarcastically said "Cute Litch."

The guys in the office clapped.

And I had another story to tell.

FAMOUS

I'm convinced that teacher's fall into one of three categories:

1% are those born to teach and spend every ounce of energy trying to be creative and make the learning process meaningful and interesting.

98% are those who once thought they were born to teach, learned otherwise, (perhaps due to unsupportive school boards, nagging parents, and seven hours of teenagers every day) and are now stuck with it; and use the same exact lesson plan year after year.

1% are those who, forgive me, are too dumb to do anything else.

My mind still argues with myself as to why Famous, as we juniors and seniors referred to him, did not fit into the last category.

He was bald, short, Italian, in love with the Latin teacher next door, and either extremely gullible or short of memory; perhaps both.

Who remembers who discovered that the top of the teacher's desk was not bolted to the frame; the part with the drawers? The names are not important. Who came up with the idea that if two guys lift up the top and two guys spin the bottom around, that when Famous came back from lunch the top of the desk would appear just as he had left it; but when he reached for the drawers—they would be gone. I am willing to take some of the credit. Read once that "there is no limit to how much a man can do if he doesn't care who gets the credit." At least three or four other guys deserve most of the credit.

He came back from lunch still hungry for the Latin teacher next door; told us all to sit down, which was unnecessary. We were already seated; we couldn't wait. He sat down and reached for a drawer and Lord didn't we think it was funny. It was. It was funny that day, and the next day and what must have been a hundred days thereafter. Every day he would come back to the room all goggled eyed, tell us to sit down and then reach for that drawer. Then he would order four goodie two shoes who had absolutely nothing to do with the crime to "march up here and put it back the way it was," much to the delight of the rest of the class. And all the time he was yelling something about immaturity, and growing up, and how the reason we come to school was to learn.

His classroom was on the second floor of the new wing, over the music rooms below. From it you looked down on the paved courtyard that served as the kindergarten playground.

It was late May. Warm enough to have the windows wide open. Warm enough that everyone's mind was a hundred miles away. We turned the desk. He took the bait as usual. He started the lecture as usual, and his face got redder and redder as the goodie two shoes did their thing. All was as usual when all of a sudden from the back of the room in the aisle near the window John started to yell; he yelled right back at Famous. "Damn it I can't take it anymore. Every day shouting, yelling, and treating us like a bunch of GD idiots just because you want to have lunch with Miss big boobs next door rather than watch your room. I can't take it anymore!" He spoke with anger, fast and heated. Did he even know what he was saying? It was bad, but what happened next was worse. To this day it is implanted in my mind like a slow motion bad accident movie.

One scuffed up brown work shoe stepped up on the seat. Its mate stepped on the desktop, and then it was on the window ledge; and suddenly John was gone.

For a moment there was stunned silence. Then girls screamed and some cried "Oh God" and someone else "Oh Nooooooo." Famous turned white and then almost in mass everyone ran to the window; so many shoving and pushing that not one could get their head out the window to view the corpse on the black top twenty feet below.

Tears came to my eyes. I just sat there. It was a joke. Just a joke on dumb Famous that's all. That jackass he should have never let it get this far. Nobody was to get hurt. Nobody was to die. John didn't have anything to do with it; he was just a farm kid. Hell he didn't have a thing to do with it. "John, why. Why, John"

John, why—are you walking through the door on your tip toes? Tough kid John is that really you waking behind the crowd at the window. "He is going to do it. He is really going to do it."

Farm kid John had jumped down twenty feet to the pavement as easily as jumping from the high beam into the hay mow of his Dad's barn. Farm kid John had popped through the music room window so fast the band teacher hardly had time to notice, He ran down the hall by the wood shop, up the stairs and was about to put his hand on Famous's shoulder and ask "what you looking for?"

John became one of the boys that day. John's parents got a letter. John got detention and a seat away from the window. I graduated in 1958 and Famous, died young a few years later. I think God figured he had suffered enough.

Get Your Own

Two or three days before Christmas after dragging a nine year old with $7.46, an eight year old with $4.32 all in loose change, and a six year old with seventeen cents and two shiny ones that Grandma had given her, through a crowded Oakdale Mall in Johnson City for the purpose of buying fifty presents for "Mommy, and you daddy," and for Aunts and Uncles, cousins and teachers and Robbie next door "because she is my friend, Daddy," I told the clerk I would just write a check.

She said "I need a license."

I told her to "Go take a test."

THE HILL

When you come right down to it, it is appalling how ill versed the general public is in its knowledge of the technical advances made in the art and science of manure distribution during the past seventy years, and the impact it has made on public safety.

Today manure is a sophisticated product, packaged and sold for a fortune from pallets in front of grocery stores to urban garden fanatics. I'm old enough to remember when it was just plain cow s—t. It still is; just with a fancy cover.

In its raw form some of it is now housed in special structures and allowed to ferment; generating methane gas as a by-product. Then it is made into slurry and once liquefied is sprayed, mind you, over the fields of dear mother earth.

When I worked on the farm you used a manure fork and strong back to lift it and the accumulated bedding from the drop; and then puffed and swore at the whole matted mess as you tossed it into the spreader. Once out on the fields you learned quickly to never engage the power take off on the tractor unless you were headed into the wind. There was a lot less chocolate splattered on your back and you tended to smell better as a result.

Mr. Prentice had a farm up the street. Nearly every night I had to walk up carrying a little pail, wait for him to finish the cow he was milking and then watched as he poured the milk through the strainer, after which he would fill my pail. We never said much. Mr. Prentice was a quiet man around kids.

Mr. Prentice liked to farm; but somehow never progressed to where he was really comfortable with a tractor and manure spreader. Mr.Prentice had a wagon and a pair of draft horses at least a zillion hands high. Mr. Prentice forked the stuff on the wagon and he forked it off, unless the snow was so high that even the horses couldn't pull his manure wagon; in which case he used a wheelbarrow and made a mountain of the stuff out behind the barn.

Some years he never made a mountain. Some years we only had a little snow. A lot of snow or a little snow, Mr. Prentice still owned the best fields around for sledding; and the quiet man never stopped us kids from enjoying our rides.

Santa Claus treated us good every year, but this year was better than most. The Christmas tree was in the corner of the living room away from the heater. The blue lights on it gave it a special luster and at four in the morning when I slipped downstairs under the pretense of having to go to the bathroom, I saw the best gift of the year leaned up against the wall. It was a full foot and a half taller than I with a dark board in the middle and two dark boards along each edge. The curved front was secured with ropes that ran down each side the full length just right for steering.

The Litchko boys were the only ones on the street who now had a toboggan save for the girls next door. We were still young enough that they didn't count just because they were girls. (Those feelings were to change in years to come.) The rest of the gifts were lost, not even remembered, due to the anticipation of a run down Prentice's hill. At Mass that morning there were lots of whispers between us and the Shiel boys about what we got and how Brother Dick and I might let them use it, once. Father Donnley may have given a two minute sermon, but boy it seemed like it lasted half a day. Then we had to stay dressed up and wait for all of the relatives to come and see us looking nice "for just once." Finally we were free to go. Like cows being let out of the barn for the first time each spring; we jumped with our long john's on, old jeans, stocking cap, a blue Navy pea jacket and new lined gloves with a hole for each finger instead of those "kids" mittens.

Across Doolittle's lawn, through the barbed wire fence; up over the knoll, along the ridge; sweating from the climb, noses cold, breath smoking as we chugged our way to the top. The snow was perfect; only about three inches of the kind that crunched. Not that wet kind that would have stuck to the bottom of the toboggan. At last we were at the top, ready for the ride of our lives; on a hill so long and so steep with enough bumps that you could not see the bottom.

First came the big brother instructions, my telling Dick, "No matter what, lean right, even if it slows down. If we go under the fence it will take our heads off. You sit in front." I was older and figured why should the family lose two heads; with him in front I might have time to duck. Scarves were wrapped around our faces up over our noses. Top buttons were buttoned up near our necks to keep the snow spray out. Dick is on with his knees pulled up under his chin so that after I gave a push and jumped on I could quickly tuck my feet in around him. Hands on Dick's shoulder I give a push. Four or five steps and I jump on. We slow for a moment and push with our hands and then just over the brink, we start to move, move faster. Move really fast. "Lean right, keep leaning right, YAAAAAHOOOOOO."

When Mr. Prentice spread manure, by hand, he spread it in lumps; not in a slurry like they do today; no little pellets like the urban gardeners use. Nope; Mr. Prentice just tossed it out there in lumps.

When the temperature drops below freezing there is no such thing as hot shit. There are just frozen lumps.

‘Lean right. Lean left. Watch it.”

The dark boards on a toboggan crack just as easy as the white ones. The bleeding on shins and chins stops after a while. And the two Litchko boys who once tobogganed on Prentice’s hill maintained a sincere interest in manure distribution long after giving up the sport.

Scars

My whole body is covered with scars. Scars, not from emergency operations or achieved in acts of bravery. No, for most part they are scars from stupidity.

There are white marks on my lower right cheek where Kozlowski's three legged German Sheppard grabbed hold of me and my bicycle seat, just because I kept ridding closer and closer to his drive way. "Public road," I said. Dog taught me where it turned private.

There is a white half moon over my right eye where I squeezed off a Winchester 32 Special when laying down and was a bit too close to the scope; wanted to show son Brian how to get a wood chuck up on the old Root farm.

There are white lines on all of my knuckles from when our canoe got slammed against the rocks while running a gorge during the Olympic trials. (A story in itself—later—later)

There is another line of dots on a finger on my left hand from when putting on a cedar shake roof using a roofer's hammer/ hatchet; I absentmindedly forgot which end to pound with. Doc Meyers in Mansfield, Texas explained the difference while he sewed.

There is a long white patch on one shim as a result of tripping over a stack of cinder blocks behind St, Mary's hall in Kirkwood, NY. It was pitch dark, around ten o'clock at night, and I was going to be "the" chaperon who caught the guys who were sneaking beer into the youth dance via the girls bathroom window. They won; I hobbled around for a week.

And there are a couple dozen microscopic prick marks that you can't see on each arm where I have given five or six gallons of blood over the past fifty years.

I suspect there is a biblical verse to cover the difference in these scars. "Your stupidity will show forever and your good deeds will only be known by God; and of course the Red Cross."

Mary's Place

My maternal grandparents had six children: over how many years I never stopped to figure; it was never important to me.

My mother is the only surviving daughter; the rest were all boy's, men actually—my Uncles; really four of my best friends. Uncle Joe, my godfather, was a perfect supplement to my Dad.

My Dad taught me to respect and love the woods. His every Sunday afternoon walks, even after we owned a TV, were important. Not just for learning about old stone walls, traces of old sheep farms, and the difference between a hard maple and sugar maple. "Remember the "U" in the leaf stands for sugar." The importance of the walks was realized later in life when the pressures of managing aerospace programs, raising a family, and paying the bills required that I find an outlet. Some men turn to golf, some to the bottle; my Dad taught me to turn to the woods.

My Uncle Joe taught me, among a ton of other things, to turn to the water, Uncle Joe liked to fish. Give me a loaf of rye bread loaded with caraway seeds, some hard salami cut thick with a sharp blade, (Uncle Joe owned his own meat market in Windsor), some sort of craft that could float with only moderate leaks from Harpursville to Windsor, my Uncle Joe for company and I was in seventh heaven. Today godfathers tend to take their roles as that of being a figurehead. My Uncle Joe set an example for all godfathers; he spent time with me.

When it came to fishing Uncle Joe was a patient man and many a day we would come off the river just below the old Windsor Bridge at ten o'clock at night yelling for Aunt Mary to get the camera and take a picture of the tonnage. Looking back it might have been a little dumb; who the hell ever enjoyed cleaning a hundred rockies, yellow bellies, small mouths and maybe a walleye or two, after you have been sitting in a canoe for ten hours. But just in case you get the urge the red Shakespeare reel is still on the rod Carole bought forty years ago and it has been used every year since. Uncle Joe may now be in heaven, but whenever he finds his closed faced Zebco we can still give it a shot.

Fishing with Uncle Joe was exciting for a number of reasons. Where are we going? Up river, down river; over to Hancock to catch eels in the Delaware so that we can make eel chips for the crew at Ma Turners hotel and maybe get a couple of free beers. Up to Cannonsville for trout, Hilltop for crappies, near Ouaquaga Creek or Fly Pond to spear suckers during the spring run. Fishing with Uncle Joe was a lesson in geography to say nothing of ecology; for example:

We might get thirsty on our way to the East Branch of the Delaware and be forced to stop at a bar in Cadosia; so remote that may of the locals didn't know it existed. Mary's bar was up near Snake Creek; I'm talking fifty years back, but it might still be there. Most unlikely that the State Liquor Authority or the IRS could ever find it. Between the condition of the road, the steep hill and the rattlesnakes for which the creek was named, they would hardly find it worth the effort. But Uncle Joe knew of this gem and he took me there on occasion.

Mary's was a big old house with a veranda across the front; six or seven stairs right in the center of the veranda got you from the stone walk to the bar entrance. Problem was that an old pickup truck was always backed right up to the stairs. To get in you had to climb up over stones to clear the tailgate and reach the edge of the third step; then haul yourself up, and with a huff you might make it to the porch. By the time you got to the door you were ready for a beer.

The outside of Mary's was lacking in décor, but it was way ahead of the inside. There was a long bar across the back and a round upright cooler with a glass door; might have had a "Gibbons" sign on it. There were ten or twelve bar stools, none of which matched and some implements that were used as tables.

Service was excellent. You just said "beer, please" and presto, there it was. No sense in asking for a brand because often at Mary's there only was one brand. Never had to worry about a dirty glass; Mary didn't give you a glass. She would just whip out her church key, ask for thirty-five cents, and lay a can on you. Never an argument about when you had "enough" at Mary's. When you finished the can you threw it through the double doors into the back of the pickup truck.

Remember me mentioning ecology? Mary had a forty year jump on the recycling fad. If you got the can through the open double doors and into the truck she would set you up again. If you got it out the door and somewhere out on the veranda she would set you up with a warning. Mary was not prone to bending over and picking up cans any more then she had to; had you ever seen her bend over you would understand that we weren't prone to having her bend over any more than she was. If the can bounced off the door jams, or worse yet the wall near the door; you were finished for the night. Although witnessed only once; if the can happened to hit somebody you were probably in for a fight; abet a very short fight because Mary never really lost control.

Sometimes if was fun to nurse a beer, sit on the side and watch the cycle; seven o'clock into the truck. Nine o'clock, on the veranda, and—if you stayed that long—off the wall.

Fishing with Uncle Joe was both exciting and educational.

Just Not Good

The worst invention in the past forty years, the one having the most detrimental effect on mankind, has been the clear top and see through plastic tackle box. Some well intended, but short sighted, do-gooder figured that if a fisherman could see through his tackle box he would be organized. (Almost ruined fishing with that thought) Figured he would know when to buy hooks, sinkers and the like, and if he had the equipment he could spend more time fishing.

Look what really happened:

First of all some poor suckers got so caught up in organization that they couldn't relax anymore. Not enough to have a few lures and a pole. No, now it's go for efficiency; get more fishing time. You have to have a pole for each lure in order to save rigging time. And of course you have to work more overtime, or get a second job, in order to afford more poles; which of course reduces fishing time. And then if you are old and forgetful you start to slip on technique when you do fish and that increases STRESS. All because some so and so invented the see through tackle box.

Second it took the "damn" out of fishing. Yes, I said damn and I meant damn, an important soul saving word for a fisherman. When you had an old metal tackle box, twenty or thirty years old, or a wonder bucket, like Uncle Joe's, (he always wondered what was in it), you never knew what you had or when you were going to run out. When you got to the river or lake you could say "Damn, I'm out of hooks, or damn I'm out of sinkers." Damn was a good stress relieving word, that you could put some emphasis behind and when it left your lips it took some of your stress with it. "Damn, I'm out of something" was a humbling sort of phrase, sort of like going to confession. When a fisherman says "Damn, I'm out of something," he is admitting he committed a fisherman's sin; he is not infallible. It is indeed a good soul searching word and much more acceptable than the language I hear from some teenagers on the streets today.

Thirdly, when you don't run out of things you can't say to your buddy, "Marlowe, you gotta hook?" Pretty soon you forget your dependence on things like community and the joy of helping one another. You start thinking that you are in complete control and don't need anyone else; you can handle it alone. You get a little uppity and stop talking to your buddy; next thing you know you are doomed to the fires of hell for being insensitive the needs of mankind. All because some son of a gun invented the plastic see-through tackle box.

The Devil In Church

I never needed sixty minutes to convince me that the devil operated in God's building. I even know the vehicle he uses. I remember eating breath mints on the way to the communion rail just to see the look on the priest's face when I stuck out a green tongue.

I recall kneeling down before Mass and running my finger through the back of Alice's neck and having her whisper, slightly annoyed, "What are you doing?" "I'm looking for hickies," I replied. And the whole congregation looked up when she said "Damn you Don."

Or, when I would sit up in the choir loft of the old Saint Mary's church in Kirkwood on Easter Sunday so that I could giggle at girls trying to walk on high heels for the first time in public; and secretly wishing one of them would get a heel stuck in the central heating grates spaced in the main aisle.

And on Palm Sunday after the distribution of palms, sitting there, putting the palm over my shoulder and leaning way back; hoping it would be sliding up the nose of the person behind me; taking great pleasure in the thought, even if I never connected.

Bless me Father for I have sinned. "I have only missed Sunday Mass six or seven times in the past seventy years; but there were a few times when I was there, that I wasn't.

Shopping At The Giant

In Binghamton, New Work, on Court Street, across from what was once the old Sears store there was a grocery store called the Giant. Pat Hastings was one of the managers, and a gal by the name of Marge was a cashier I trusted before the days of bar coding and scanning. There were other Giant stores in Binghamton; but the Court Street Giant was the ONLY one as far as I was concerned.

Grocery shopping can be a depressing, however necessary, function. It is expensive; takes time out of the week; and heaven help us, through the frustration of sorting through coupons, waiting in lines, carts with one wheel that won't roll, and back then paper sacks that break open between the car and the house; but only on rainy days or when the snow was four feet deep. The Giant on Court Street didn't solve all those problems, but it somehow made the whole process more tolerable.

For one thing it never changed. I went in the store once five years after having moved to Texas and found everything just the way I had left it. The Hansmann's pancake flower was right where it was supposed to be, The big bin with the empty cartons was there so you could pick one up for the heavy stuff; or even "borrow" a few boxes to make Halloween costumes if you so needed. And best of all was the "help;" who all seemed to remember me.

I know because when I walked in I heard one of them say "OH God—they are back." Down deep I knew just where she was coming from and it felt good. I was a regular Friday night or Saturday morning shopper, but so were hundreds of others. I usually paid by check, but so did hundreds of others. The element of distinction, the thing that separated me from everyone else, was that for fifteen years I shopped with four kids; and the older they got the more fun we had; so much in fact that Carole, my wife, refused to go in with us, Bet they don't remember Carole at the Giant.

When they were young, it was fitting three in the cart, carrying one in my LL Bean pack basket and going through the aisles with eight little hands reaching, grabbing and putting things I didn't want into the cart. When they got older they began to realize that Daddy would not let their picks make it to the casher's counter. They also noticed that rather than walk back and return the items to the shelf where they belonged daddy would just slip them into someone else's cart when they weren't looking. With four kids it really saved me a lot of time. By the time they were eight, nine, and ten, the game became how much stuff could they put in other peoples carts; and who could keep the straightest face at the checkout line when some old buzzard would ask his wife, "What the hell you buying that for?"

Then we figured out how to speed up the buying process by employing the "give every kid their own cart" trick. Dad would run the loop around the perimeter and each kid was assigned a specific aisle. It was easy to monitor their progress as I worked the outside edges; just had to listen to their comments ring through the store; Squuuuuuuse me lady," "Watch it," "Move it Grandma." Sometimes a voice I didn't recognize would chime in with a "Whose kid is that?" And there was the weekly yell from aisle four "Dad, do we need toilet paper?" Once we bought a hundred and twenty dollars worth of stuff in nine minutes with no duplicates and three coupons. The Litchko kids knew about team work.

Sometimes the store would be real busy and there were not enough carts; so to help we would run the five man—three aisle at a time play. The youngest kid would push the cart up aisle two. Next youngest would walk ahead of the cart and do the picking from aisle two. I'd walk behind the pusher and act as catcher. One kid would work aisle one and one aisle three. On signal we walked down the aisles together. 'Hey Dad" and a box of Cheerios would come through the air from aisle three. "Yo Pop," and some cucumbers would sail over from the veggie aisle. Fifteen years we never lost an item or dropped anything glass.

"Single file on the conveyor belt was another simple but fun game. Never did figure why people pile, stack, cram, and stuff all the purchases on the checkout conveyor at once; the cashier can only handle one thing at a time! I do know that if you want to get a lot of weird looks try putting your items on the conveyor single file—one item at a time. You can really tick some people off; even cashiers will give you the "what's this" look. I have had people swear and switch lines because they think it takes longer when I place items on one at a time than it does the cashier to ring them up—one item at a time.

Yep; after five years the folks at the Giant remembered me.

Shopping With Mildred

Went grocery shopping with Mildred once; she was a co-worker whose spirit I always enjoyed; our task was to pick up items for an office party. I looked at a particular brand of pickles and asked her if they were any good. Millie took the bottle off the shelf; gave the lid a twist, removed it and held the jar up to her nose. “Smells good,” she said and then replaced the cover and returned the jar to the shelf.

“Well then let’s get one.” Millie reached over and took the jar adjacent to the one she just put back.

“What was wrong with the first one?” I asked.

“It had already been opened, “said she.

(after laughing we bought the opened one)

There Is Always One

I like to sing. Not the greatest; not the worst, and have sang in church choirs for the past fifty—five years—all over the country; and have noticed that in every singing group there is always "one."

When someone took Grandma's old flat iron and added a wire to it every woman in the world endorsed the change. When someone put a tea kettle inside the iron to make steam, they loved it. When a plastic tube was added so that one could see how much water was in the iron they all sang "Ode to Joy." And when Teflon was added on the iron face so that it would not stick, from every laundry room, almost in unison, we heard "Hallelujah, keep those changes coming."

Why then, if women like change, have I never sung in a group without one woman saying "stop, stop, that's not the way it was written?" The Struggling Men's Choir was an all men's choir. We made beautiful music; were often invited to sing at other parishes—and darn if we didn't have a woman stop me once and tell me "that was nice, but it's not the way it was written."

Just because somebody invented a song doesn't mean that we can't add or subtract a note here or there; draw a tail on a bubble or two, color in the holes and add fins to the little space ships and maybe improve the song in the process.

The next time some woman tells me "that's not the way it was written," I'm going to take her iron back.

A Slice Off The Old Block

Uncle Joe and Aunt Mary owned the only real meat market in Windsor, New York. There were other stores and they were nice, but there was only one Urda's "WINDSOR MARKET." It was a two aisle store. The cash register and check out was on your right as you walked in with all the cigarettes and candy bars right behind the cashier. Aunt Mary was the chief cashier and that way she could be certain that little items would not disappear from the shelves, if you know what I mean. On the left was the bread rack.

Then there was the long meat case with rolls and rolls of sandwich meat, pans of liver, trays of roasts, steaks, pork chops, chickens and all sort of good stuff in between. At the end of the aisle was the chopping block where Uncle Joe would flash his knife along the steel and then yield his cuts. If you wanted a three and a half pound roast he would eyeball the chunk of meat, make a slice and then beam from ear to ear when it was placed on the scale and no trimming was necessary. Uncle Joe sort of had an eye for meat.

During the summer months a lot of Jewish customers vacationed in the area. (The Catskills were known as the Jewish Alps back then) they would come into the market knowing they were a long way from the Kosher markets of their native New York City; the men would point to a chicken and say "Kosher" Joe. Kosher in Windsor, New York meant the Uncle Joe would give his knife at least two quick wipes in his apron; then with the help of his trusty clever that bird was quarter and into pieces before the customer could change his mind.

I cut a Kosher chicken once. Uncle Joe was busy with another customer when a regular Jewish customer walked by, pointed to a chicken and said 'Kosher Joe." Uncle Joe just said 'Donnie," and nodded towards the chicken; it was my debut, time to show my stuff. Knife in my right hand I went swish, swish on my white apron. I grabbed that bird with confidence and placed it on the block. The cleaver split the backbone on the first try; never even came close to a finger. The wings and rest were separated just as though it was Uncle Joe swinging the implements. I had studied well. While demonstrating my wrapping talents and knot tying skills I did sense there might be something wrong; my jeans felt sticky.

As soon as the customer left I was on my way to the wash room behind the cooler. Apparently I needed a little more practice with the swish, swish, in the apron routine. I had swished through the apron, through my jeans and neatly slice my thigh.

Uncle Joe had a lifelong career as a meat cutter. I added another scar to my collection and became a manufacturing engineer.

● ● ● ● ●

I Love

The person who wrote the lyrics "I love little baby ducks, old pickup trucks, slow moving trains and rain" must have known me in a previous life.

Old pickup trucks are special; they have special smells; the smell of a sun baked and winter frozen seat cover that is now so cracked that you can see the stuffing through the imitation leather. The smell of oil that spilled on the floor from that half filled can that you forgot was there; the smell of gasoline from the containers that were placed up front when the bed was full of junk. And of course the smell of dirt that was once on your shoes; and the hair of the dog that always rode with his head out the window.

On a true old pickup truck the dash board is dry and hard; sprinkled with spots from coffee cups that were placed there on cold winter mornings while waiting for buddies to come out of the woods; or from beer cans shared with fishing partners. The odometer has been stuck on 110376 miles for a couple of years; and the needle on the speedometer doesn't need to work because nobody wants to go fast in an old pickup truck. Beside in a real, old, pickup truck you can look down through the rusted floor board on the driver's side and watch the little stones on the tar fly by in a blur and you can kind off judge your speed if ever necessary.

The steering wheel of an old pickup truck is covered with an accumulation of grim except in those one or two spots where you just naturally grab the wheel when you bend over to turn on the key, or hold on while driving.

Radios don't work in old pickup trucks unless the antenna has been replaced with a bent up coat hanger. Even then it works so bad that you don't mind turning it off and singing to yourself, or being quiet and having thoughts. Many a problem can be solved when driving alone in an old pick up truck.

There is always a crescent wrench on the floor and sometime a wooden handled screw driver. A loose spare tire is in the back that bounces with a thud when you hit a bump and it slides back and forth when you round a curve or turn a corner.

You are never inhibited in an old pickup truck. You are high enough that you can look down on people who are driving Cadillac's, with their noses up. You can spit out the window and not worry that it will splatter on the back window. You dare go anywhere because another dent, another scratch just won't matter. And if it dies, for what it's worth, you can just walk away. But once you have owned one it is like a family member. It may go away but it is always yours.

Daughters when you marry; don't deny him a pile of rust in the driveway; it's a small price to pay for his happiness.

And Sons, may you never be so successful, so fast, that you never have the need to own an old pickup truck.

Documented Jackass

Instinctively I knew the ankle was going to hurt even before my foot hit the ground. The basket ball went out of bounds and I went to the hospital.

During the follow up visit the doctor suggested that while twenty-six was not old, in view of the fact that the ankle had been injured repeatedly, it might be prudent to give up contact sports. "Don you will pay for it in years to come."

Seven weeks later it was necessary to pay him another visit as a result of a similar injury during a game between the local state troopers and the team from Saint Mary's in Kirkwood. This time he was a little more adamant.

"I told you to stop; what are you a complete jackass? If you ever come in here again with a sports injury I won't even work on you."

Years pass. We visit friends in Ottawa. After a brief sprinkle type shower our host, Bob, suggested we go outside and play catch with the kids Nerf football. It was a short pass, and my leather soles were slippery. I was horizontal to the ground the moment just prior to breaking my wrist. (Just chipped a bone)

Back in the states I went to the same doctor's office. Seems he had died and a young man had taken over his practice. He asked if I had even been there before and then went for my file.

"How did you break your wrist?"

"Catching a football."

"'You are a jackass."

"How do you know?"

"Says so right here. Sports injury must be complete jackass."

Many have thought it; a few have said it; but Doc Brown was the only one to document it. I hope.

● ● ● ● ●

I'M ON IT

I was waiting at the gate in LaGuardia. He was drunk; a happy drunk, but definitely drunk. His wit and bantering with fellow travelers, the agent at the gate, and even with the pilots as they walked toward the ramp amused most of us. As we lined up to board by rows, he positioned himself right next to the agent who was collecting the boarding passes and said to each passenger, "Hope you have a safe flight." The old battleaxe ahead of me looked like she had voted for prohibition. She gave him a most disgusted look and said coldly, "WHY."

Without hesitation he answered, "Because I'm on it."

Pop Kinney

One of the blessing of coming from a large family was that I had uncles who had attend the same high school as I; just a few years previous. Uncle Fred like the physics and chemistry teacher, Pop Kinney. I liked Uncle Fred, so it was natural that I liked Pop Kinney; long before I ever took physics.

Uncle Fred had taught me the law of the lever, the inclined plane, and the right hand rule for polarity long before I got to high school. His nephew was going to shine when he got to Pop Kinney's class. Had he taught me not to say "Good morning, Pop" on my first day of class I would have got off to a much better start.

Uncle Fred had also taught me that Pop could knock a fly off your nose with a piece of chalk from twenty feet out, if he had a mind to. When provoked by inattention, Pop would slowly walk the length of the black board, dragging his eraser in the dust try. Talking as he walked back and forth was his style; then at the proper moment, wham, that eraser would hit the inattentive in the chest so hard that after two washings there would still be chalk dust in his shirt. Uncle Fred's lessons were seldom wasted on me.

Jerry sat behind me and had been on my case for two or three days; putting me down every chance he got. It was time to apply lessons learned. Next Physics class I started to fidget, whisper, and get Pop's attention. He gave me the "look" and then, just like Uncle Fred had said, he started that slow walk the length of the black board, dragging the eraser. When he got near his desk I deliberately turned my head to give him the proper opportunity. It was perfect. Pop let go and I hit the floor. I was taller than Jerry so my chest was about where his head was; and that was where the eraser hit him; right in the head.

I was the first one to have to stand outside the Physics Class door that year. I don't think Jerry ever like me much, but never made an issue of it after that. Pop told me after class that it was the first time he ever missed. I assured him that he hadn't lost his touch and explained that I had taken unfair advantage of him. Also told him I was too full of vengeance to have very much remorse. He smile; and Pop and I became friends.

● ● ● ● ●

Lessons By George

Uncle Fred was not my only teacher. Uncle George was capable of passing on a little wisdom now and then; things like:

"There would be fewer divorces if everyone had to get a learners permit before they were issued a marriage license."

And

"No state should discriminate by having a minimum drinking age. Every young man should have the same opportunity to make a jackass out of himself as his father does."

Tale Of Two Cities

My disappointment with the movie "The Tale of Two Cities," was directly attributable to the distance between my grandmother's chicken coup and her chicken soup.

When you walked out of my Grandma's kitchen door you looked directly at the wood shed. Between the she and the house, and continuing out to the drive was a slab stone sidewalk. Today we know those slabs to be the much desired and rather expensive Susquehanna Blue stone; back in those days it was just nice big flat stones. In between the stones and down on the end near the driveway my Dad and Uncles would, from time to time, shovel in some shale to reduce the mud and dirt that would normally track into the house. Those big flat stones were my blackboards. By taking a small sharp stone I could scratch pictures all day long and never run out of space. Normal foot traffic and occasional rain showers were my erasers. I learned how to play tick-tac-toe on those stones. The shale was my sand box. An old spoon, with my imagination became a steam shovel. A curved rock made for a pretend bulldozer. And flat stones became dump trucks. Enough highways, tunnels, bridges and access roads were built along that sidewalk to rival all of today's interstates.

The woodshed was a long, lean-to type roof, unpainted wood structure that ran two thirds the length of the house. The shed floor was half wood planks and half dirt; but only someone who lived there would know because the dirt was covered with years of accumulated wood ships. More often than not the shed had that special smell that can only come from fresh split wood. There was a big anvil that would ring like a church bell when I hit it with my grandfather's ball peen hammer. As pleasant a sound as it was to my ears, not all found it so. The words "Donnie, stop that" would frequently flow out of the house after ten minutes of my pounding. There were warped wooden shelves mounted to the walls that held a few old fishing lures, and a chrome plated casting reel with mother of pearl handles. Hung on one wall was an all steel fishing pole. There was also a long stemmed oil can that could squirt for a mile when you pushed the dimpled bottom. I was always careful to squirt it on the dirt floor and then cover it up with wood chips so as to prevent getting yelled at for wasting the oil. There is a lot of oil in that dirt. There was also my Uncle Fred's best and only baseball glove, the one he let me use for my first Little League game.

Grandpa Urda use to like to sit in an old banged up kitchen chair, with his back to the shed and watch his boys throw curve balls, knuckle balls and sliders; each son thinking how someday he would be the next Whitey Ford, or maybe get a shot at playing for the Triplets; that Yankee Triple A farm team that played in Johnson City. (While all the guys in the family liked baseball I don't think Grandma Urda ever understood it; if everyone was crouched near the radio listening to the World Series, and it was time to do chores before milking, she would start hollering "BULL PEN—BULL PEN" out in the kitchen.)

There was a small ditch around the shed to divert water from rains and spring thaws. On one end of the shed was a wooden rain barrel with rusty metal rings around it. It was the barrel my brother Dick fell against one night when trying to hide during a game of kick the can; "Ooooley, Oooley in free." And so it was that while Dick was rushed down to Doc Stillson's office the rest of the family prayed he would live. The cut was near his temple.

There was a path on the end of the shed that led up a small incline to the chicken coup. In between the coup and the shed was a small clump of locust trees whose wood was prized for fence posts. Locust is not quick to rot even when set in wet ground. Young locust trees had sharp barbs on their trunks shaped like sharks teeth, that a six year old could pry and break off; then he could sneak up on a Dad or Uncle, whoever was taking a Sunday afternoon nap and stick it in their bottom. It was a way of livening up lazy Sunday afternoons and letting the rest of the family know that I was a little bored.

Grandma's chicken soup got its start in the barn red chicken coup; that's where she keep her chicken stock, if you can get my drift. The candidate chicken would be chased, separated from the flock, cornered and caught amid a whole bunch of loud squawking and wing flapping. Never once did a chicken walk over and say "Oh, what the heck, it must be my turn;" they all offered serious protest.

Once caught, the chicken would be carried by its legs, out to the chopping block and its head detached by use of a hatchet. This part of the chicken soup process was never very pleasant, but, on the other hand, it was never very long either.

No matter how loud the thud or how sad the detachment, the next step of the process never failed to amuse me. The beheaded chicken would be let go and immediately it would run around the yard bumping into locust trees (presumably due to its now poor eyesight,) and then would do a little dance with much wing flapping before finally biting the dust. Having watched the process from the time I was a little tot it was well ingrained by the time I was nine or ten.

You did not have to be the best reader in the second grade, (I was the best reader in the slow readers group, according to Mrs. Webster; who was no relation to the dictionary clan,) to know that the Saturday night movie listed in the Windsor Standard did not include Roy Rogers, Hop-a-long Cassidy, Gene Autry, or the Lone Ranger. I had no desire to see the "Tale of Two Cities" until Uncle Dave explained the workings of a guillotine. Uncle Dave, in his youth, had a flare for the exciting things in life. I consented to see the show and stopped whining about the lack of cowboys. I figured that if chickens dance when beheaded then humans, being bigger, ought to really put on a show. Why maybe I could even guess the nationalities of the victims. If she danced a polka she was probably Polish; if he dance a waltz, perhaps Austrian, and so on and so forth. It didn't take much imagination to get me really into looking forward to the event.

The movie dragged on for hours; all words and no action. I slumped down in my seat and pressed my feet against the back of the seat in front of me, to the annoyance of its occupant. My mother slapped my feet and told me to sit up and "please" let her enjoy the show. Then finally, after forever, it happened.

The two of them climbed the stairs and were made to kneel down and place their heads in the yoke. A prayer was said, just long enough to let the anticipation build, and then WHOMP; the big blade did its job. And then, "nothing," not a damned thing.

The Tale of Two Cities was one big disappointment; they just weren't chicken enough.

◉ ◉ ◉ ◉ ◉

Three Out Of Ten Is Not Bad

Father was desperate when he asked me to substitute teach the Religious Ed class after Mass that morning; the regular teacher had not showed up.

With no time to prepare I dragged out taking attendance and then decided the best way to keep them under control was to give a surprise test. "List the Ten Commandments," was followed by a brief moment of panic; I could only remember nine.

The first sheet handed in read:

Honor Mother and Father

Don't swear

Don't shack up with neighbor's wife.

He may not have known the letter of the law, but he sure captured the intent.

If Only You Had Been There

In general I really like family parties and, in general, especially now being one, I enjoy old folks; be they gentle and loving, or ornery and cantankerous. Cousin Dawn's anniversary party coupled both of these delights into one memorable afternoon and evening.

When the invitation announced a surprise party for Ed and Dawn it was easy to get psyched for the occasion. Dawn is a fast wit, tell like it is, person who is always ten feet ahead of the rest of the pack. She can turn a funeral into a happy occasion. Ed, her husband is the kind of guy you always liked to be around. He was always an excellent host and we looked forward to being able to do something nice for him for a change. We weren't going to this outing because we had to; "we wanted to."

The location was a restaurant in the Vestal Plaza where, according to rumor, they went every year for their anniversary. I guess he popped the question to her in this place or something like that. At any rate it was a special place for the two of them; so we were told.

Family from Ed's side and family from Dawn's side showed up early for the surprise as if of one accord. Everyone was giddy before they even had a drink; all saying, "Won't they be surprised?" Tables were decorated, presents stacked high, and the drinks and fellowship flowed; so much so that nobody cared that Ed and Dawn were a little late. Another drink or two and now the couple are an hour late. We laughed about how

Dawn must have gotten wind of it and was probably sitting out in the parking lot laughing at us. Well the laugh would be on her because we were having a darn good time without her. Another drink or two and now the restaurant manager is concerned about dried out Ziti and Ravioli, and sixty people milling around who were definitely not dried out.

We were definitely in the party mood when surprise, surprise, the organizer announced with tear filled eyes, that she just found out she had set up the whole affair in the wrong restaurant. Embarrassed she calls the right restaurant, their home, their friend's home. No Dawn and Ed. Dawn and Ed missed the best darn anniversary party they ever had.

In unison both families held their glasses high and said as of one voice, "the hell with them, let's eat."

The manager is happy. Miss organizer is apologetic; and the rest of us were more than willing to live with the situation; that was until Aunt Mary announces that "Stanley is gone."

Forgive me my family, because I'm sure it is just me, but for the first seventy years of his life I thought Uncle Stanley was the Scrooge of Christmas past. Uncle Stanley and I just never got to know each other very well, and neither of us lost much sleep over the matter. I do believe in his last five or six years, when he mellowed, we might have found a way had we tried.

"Stanley's gone," says Aunt Mary; and since one chair is empty I believe her and picked up the tablecloth to see if he is under there. My mother nudges me and says, "Watch it. She is serious. Aunt Mary is serious." After five beers the situation strikes me as humorous and I whisper back to my mother, "What's the concern; hasn't she been wishing he'd take a hike for years now." No nudge; this time my Mother hits me. My brother Dick thinks we should have another beer and discuss the matter. We did.

Scouting parties walked through every store in the Mall. The parking lot is checked. Uncle Stanley's car is inspected; but no Uncle Stanley is to be found. Speculation runs high, "He's been kidnapped!" Now people are looking under the tables in earnest. I tell my mother that "I had the jump on them an hour ago." She gives me another more earnest nudge.

To get to his house across from the Johnson City High School old Uncle Stanley had walked a couple of miles across and along the dangerous Vestal Parkway; past the sewage treatment plant, over the longest bridge in Broome County, across the busiest traffic circle in Johnson City, under the old Erie-Lackawanna railroad tracks and down several confusing streets; trudging all the way.

"Stanley, what happened?"

"I was tired of waiting; went outside for some air; forgot what restaurant you were in; so I came home." End of story.

I like family parties and old people; and I love Dawn and Ed, without whom I could never had enjoyed such a fine day.

Mutual Disrespect

I owe a lot to many professors at Broome Technical College; somehow they managed to imprint enough knowledge in me that I was able to raise and support a wonderful wife and family. There where one or two, however, that failed to impress me.

He never impressed me as a mechanics professor. Static loads, vector analysis and such were important and I enjoyed the subject; it was he who I found boring. I was day dreaming when he asked, “Litchko, why are the old roads so curvy?” I thought it was because the builders got paid by the mile. He didn’t like my reply and spent the next half hour explaining how because the roads followed old Indian paths and deer trails. We sure didn’t learn much about building bridges that day; he didn’t even discuss how they cut down trees across creeks so they could keep their feet dry when crossing.

Just Listen

The slice of redwood in the souvenir shop had these words on it; "If you aren't the lead dog the view never changes. Made me feel sorry of the Eskimos; never saw a dog sled picture in which the Eskimo was not the last one in the chain of events.

I spent most of my working life as a group leader, foreman, supervisor or manager of something or other; consequently can attest to the fact that the view does change, but often because some other dog whimpers.

This might be an appropriate time to admit publicly, in writing, what most of my co-workers always knew; that being that everyone who ever worked for me longer than a year was smarter than I was.

Ask any of them, "are you smarter than Litch?" and ninety-eight percent of them will answer "hell yes." The other two percent are either dead or find the experience to painful to talk about. Don't take a survey; I admit it; they are smarter than me.

The whole trouble with people who are smart, people who are experts, people who are most knowledgeable, is that they know so much that they know why things can't be done. "It is impossible; it can't be; there is not enough of something or other." Furthermore smart people never hesitate to tell you why it can't be done.

Ever hear of a Board of Directors hiring someone because he or she was good at telling them why something can't be done?

Never in a million years. I got to be a manager and director simply by being so ignorant as to know that something can't be done. Give me a penny for every time I have said "yep, sure, we'll take care of it," when I didn't have the faintest idea of how the hell I was going to do it, and I'd be a wealthy man today. I was always ignorant enough to think maybe there was a way; but in fact was seldom the one who figured out how to do it.

One thing I learned early in life was that there is no shortage of people who want to tell me, and you, what and how to do things. Parents, teachers, other relatives, priests and ministers, friends, neighbors, mayors, editors, coworkers and bums on the street all want to tell me "what to do."

Smart people hate to be told what to do; obviously because they think they are smart enough to know what to do without being told. Ignorant people like me thrive on being told what to do; in fact I have grown to count on it.

Boss called me in one day and with an abundance of four letter words explaining that we were losing our ass because of problems with a certain actuator; and had been for years. I told him I would look at it and that's exactly what I did. I took the part, put it on the corner of my desk, looked at it, and waited; but not for long.

Darn near everyone who walked in my office just reeked with ideas on what I should do. "What's that, Litch;" "oh just an actuator that is costing us a bundle. Wish I knew what the heck to do." That is all it took; all I had to do then was listen.

One engineer knew another engineer who knew something about the molecular structure of some new compound. I had no idea of what he was talking about but was impressed enough to jot down a few buzz words.

Another guy talked about changing the rake on a carbide drill. I thought rakes were used in gardens; but remembered just in time that I was ignorant; so I took a few notes.

The janitor volunteered that it looked like the parts he often picked up from the floor near the inspection station, "because they always stack them close to the edge and sometimes they get knocked off; of course they are metal Litch, so it doesn't matter." The tolerances on those "metal parts" were so fine that if you took the diameter of a human hair and divided it into a hundred parts and then took just one of those parts that is how much space you had between parts when you assembled that actuator. That janitor had told me a lot.

The bore machine operator bitched about how the company was "too damn cheap to buy a new fixture, so screw em they get what they deserve." He had told his manger about the fixture being borderline, close to out of tolerance; and because he was loud, arrogant, and a habitual bitcher; he was told to stop complaining and go do his job. Turned out that he was loud, arrogant, even obnoxious, and very, very, right.

To make a long story short over three weeks time sixteen different people volunteered thoughts, observations, etc. and gave me a list of twenty-eight items that could be changed to save money on that part. And fifteen of those sixteen always ended their conversations with a comment something like "but it will never change." The sixteenth guy went on to become a manager.

Things were changed; the company saved money, and I got a promotion for "having looked at it."

So my free advice to those future managers of the world is: Never be so smart that you know why things can't be done;

promotions go to those who get things done. If your people are not smarter than you, at least in their area of expertise, get rid of them. And thrive on free advice given from any source. You don't have to use it; but if it is free, why not listen?

Now About Cows

Cows are dumb, loving and lovable, just in case anybody cares. I've known a few cows and for the sake of posterity feel compelled to document my knowledge for future generations.

Every summer during my youth I would pack my bags, and, move to my grandparent's farm in Smithville Flats, NY just as soon as school was out. It was a thrill to be able to drive a tractor, ride hay wagons, swim in the Genegenslet Creek, hunt wood chucks with an old single shot twenty-two, and even milk cows.

Never saw a cow do a trick. Cows don't walk around on their front legs or stand on their heads. That's why you never see one in a circus. Cows don't fetch slippers, moo when a car pulls in the driveway, or curl up around your feet in front of the fireplace on a cold winter night. Cows make lousy house pets.

Never met a cow that was either house broken or barn broken for that matter; cows just do their thing wherever and whenever they get the urge.

The only thing about predictable about cows is that if you have just whitewashed the barn so that it is as white as the shower room at the YMCA; at least one in the herd will sneeze. And when it is done sneezing that white wall will look like Dalmations back.

A sneezing cow is nothing to sneeze at; no sir. You are okay if you are standing to the left of her. You are okay if you as standing to the right of her; but never, never stand behind her. Remember the phrase "Oh the wind blue and the s—t flew;" it was coined by someone in the know. Cows do give warning of upcoming sneezes and the novice should be alert of these signs when walking through a barn. First you hear a series of low, deep coughs; similar to those made by an alcoholic that smokes first thing in the morning. It is sad that most of you can relate better to an alcoholic than to a cow; but what can I do about that? Cows do have big lungs and can really get down there when it comes to coughing. The real signal is when they start to hunch their backs much like a mad cat. If you look down a row of cows and see even one that looks like a golden arch; stay away.

If instead of muskets and cannons Lee had lined up a hundred cows along Seminary ridge and had his quartermasters sprinkle a little pepper up their noses on command, I do believe the South would have taken Gettysburg and the national anthem today would have been "Dixie." Lee was either not aware of dairy warfare tactics, or much too much a gentleman to use them.

Typically cows are not prone to quick movements; let alone stampedes. Call "Heeeeeeaaaarrr Boss, Heeeaaare Boss, send out the dog, or go to the pasture yourself to chase them and they will still walk to the barn at one pace, "slow." If you even try to hustle them along they turn their heads and give that "if you want any milk you best get off my case look." I only know of one way to get run over by a heard of Holsteins, and darn near had it happen twice.

If the herd decides to pasture two miles from the barn be assured that the pregnant one will drop her calf four miles from the barn. If the herd is in an open pasture, she will find and deliver in the middle of a blackberry patch; I speak the truth. Finding a new calf is often a chore; abet an exciting chore. Picking up a newborn calf that has just been licked clean by its mother is a special part of being a farmer. Oh, he will moan and groan about having to go find the dumb thing; because it always happens on the night he has to go to a volunteer firemen's meeting or something like that; but if you could only hear him when he finally finds mother and child. Soft as a little girl taking to her dolls he starts whispering; "Hello girl. Oh what a fine little gal you have there, Oh don't get nervous, she is such a fine thing. I'm not going to hurt her." He means every bit of it. A new calf can turn a hayseed bully into a Saint without so much as a moment's notice.

If you think that this new Saint epitomizes love that is only because you have never seen a herd of love; you have never carried a newborn calf past the rest of the herd on the way to the barn. This is real touchy stuff. First every cow comes to look the new addition over and try to smell it. Then they all moooooo and carry on like humans looking though the glass at the maternity ward; but much more vocal. It would be fine if only it would stop there. Cows, however, develop an immediate mother's complex. The heck with all that gestation and labor stuff; all hundred and twenty of them each think that calf is hers, and all hundred and twenty of them want to walk right next to "her" calf as you walk back to the barn. Your back may hurt and your arms get dead tired but once you walk by that herd you don't put that calf down unless you want to get trampled. Cows are loving creatures but they can love you to death.

Wheat farmers are just dairy farmers that tried carrying a calf past a herd, once.

Ever seen a good painting of a cow face? What, never; know why? It is the eyes; there has never been an artist good enough to capture the beauty of a cow's eyes. Sometime stop to take a look into those big, round, droopy eyes and tell me what in the world can match them. During winter months when they were kept in the barn we would fluff up fresh hay and then sprinkle molasses on it as a treat; probably added some iron to their diet. I would be sprinkling along, minding my own business when one would start rubbing her neck up and down my overalls; then she would turn her head and roll her eyes at me and whomp, she would have me conned out of an extra pint of molasses without ever even really trying.

Milking a cow is a neat experience. Cows are neither digital nor analog. Every cow I milked operated only in the manual mode. You don't just walk up to bossy and press a button. No this is a slow, almost religious, experience.

Cows are big creatures and while they have horns they don't come with rear view mirrors. Prior to messing around with the rear end it is wise to send them some sort of a signal; most of which is body language. First you put your left hand on her back almost at the point where her tail is connected. This tells her several things: I only want white milk; I prefer that you don't kick, and please cow don't lie down while I am under you milking. With your left hand still on her back you straddle the drop, (this is where the messy stuff is,) keeping one foot out in the aisle and the other long side the cow. This is so that if she decides to kick you will still have one good foot to hop to the hospital on. With your free hand holding a warm damp cloth you bend over, balance on one foot and try to wash the four facets hanging under the udder.

Jane Fonda may look better than most farmers and she may be in great shape but I doubt she could wash and dry fifty udders and two hundred facets, while balancing on one foot without slipping into the drop at least once.

By now old bossy is expecting some action so best that you grab a clean stainless steel pail, pull up a milking stool and position yourself under the cow. This is the basic squat position; your bottom is six inches off the ground; your knees are above your head and they are squeezing the milk pail to hold it upright; freeing your hands to milk.

Next you adjust your cap. NEVER milk a cow without wearing a cap, and the cap has to be tilted with the visor down over your left eye. Think I'm putting you on? Ever been slapped with a wet towel in the locker room. Picture a three foot tail that has been soaking in a drop filled with both solid and liquid matter for half a day, wrapping you aside the head when old bossy suddenly decides she needs to swap the fabled blue tail fly.

Now grab either the front two, or the rear two, faucets and commence to work. First one faucet, than the other; developing a sing song rhythm; squeezing the finger closest to the udder and then the others in succession; while at the same giving the whole facet a gentle tug. If you are lucky you get a little squirt on the first try and you most likely will miss the pail. Repeat the process with the other hand and in a bit you will develop a rhythm.

When the pail is empty each squirt makes a ringing sound and you can change the pitch by aiming at different heights or spots on the bottom of the pail. Once the pail accumulates some milk each squirt drives a little air into the fluid and pretty soon a foam builds up; much like the head on a draft beer. Each subsequent squirt slices through the foam and makes a little swishing sound; and each swish makes you feel like a real farmer.

It has been at least forty-five years since I last milked a cow; but as I look over the heads of all the people on Flight 401, going from San Antonio to Boston, I realize that I might be the only one on this plane that could still call his city cousins over to see where the milk comes from, and then, squirt them in the eye from fifteen feet out, or hit a cats open mouth from ten.

How To Impress Hancock

I doubt if there has ever been a traffic jam in Hancock, New York. Years back, in the early evening people might congregate outside Candyland; and if they had some loose change they might go in and have a soda or buy some chunks of white chocolate. Up the street was the movie theater and nearby was Tony's where you could get a good pizza and a beer.

One certainly didn't drive from Windsor to Hancock for the exciting night life. You went to Hancock either to take Uncle Joe to see his tax man or to fish the East Bank of the Delaware. There is a big bend in the river right behind the village. If you drove across Fireman's field, (the local ball park,) you can park close to the water, wade out and catch anything that was hungry. In the upper branches of the Delaware you can catch trout, bass, shad when they are running, eels, and catfish; it is possible to catch a complete fisherman's sampler all in one night.

It was embarrassing to have the lights flash and hear the siren go off behind me just as people were exiting the last movie on Saturday night. I knew I wasn't speeding as I had given the constable a polite nod as I slowly drove across the bridge coming back in to town. I was even more embarrassed when after telling him that I had not been drinking when he insisted that I touch my nose and walk a straight line. I accomplished both tasks without difficulty. I then asked him what I could have possibly done to even suggest that I was inebriated. "Well son, in the fifteen years I have patrolled this town yours is the first car I have seen come through at midnight with a pair of hip boots standing on the roof."

He didn't lie. I had rinsed off my waders at the river's edge and then set them on the roof while I sat in the driver's seat to put on my sneakers. It was late; I was tired; so I just pulled on those size twelve's and started to drive home.

An experience like this tends to make one a bit self conscious. I still think that if I borrowed a turquoise and white fifty-six Chevy, and drove through Hancock on a Saturday night, now fifty years later, someone would yell, "That's him, that's the guy."

Litch Vs Phoenix

Prior to Cousin Rick taking his bar exams I do believe that I was the only family member who could boast of having won one hundred percent of all his cases. This I attribute to having been tenacious enough to take on the City of Phoenix; and smart enough to quit after my first trial.

I woke up from an afternoon nap with a taste for ice cream. Wearing a pair of cut off jeans, sandals, no shirt, and sporting an unshaven face and uncombed head, I drove to the nearest convenience store a couple of blocks away.

On the return trip I stopped at an intersection and saw a car a long way off to my right. I judged there was ample time to make it across and proceeded to do so. I almost made it when boom, the rear bumper on my sixty Dodge Dart took a direct hit.

The Dart had a bent bumper that I eventually had fixed for less than fifty bucks. The big, black, Chrysler Imperial that hit me did not fair as well. His repairs would exceed three hundred dollars. Remember, in those days you could buy a new car for four thousand, or so. His damages were significant.

The police came, took one look at Mr. Business suit and another look at young Mr. Cutoffs and sandals and only one of us got a ticket for not yielding to the right of way. I was guilty by appearance. I was also very irritated. No, I was not irritated; I was PO'd.

It was a mail in fine, definitely a case where it would be cheaper to pay than to fight. Even in those days I could have afforded the ten dollars; but even in those days a young driver with a mark on his license could expect an insurance increase come next renewal period.

Required spending two nights at the library reading statutes and making copies; I pulled up to officers parked on street corners and asked some "what if" questions. I was actually able to find out that the officer who issued the ticket had only been on active duty for two weeks. It took another half day to go to court, plead not guilty and request a jury trial. That request was denied. The judge thought he could handle it without their help. Took still another day to make certain the witnesses I wanted called were issued a subpoena. I took a vacation day to sit in the back of a courtroom and watch how things were done. This was a long time before Judge Judy and LA Law.

Time means nothing when you are twenty-two, tenacious, and PO'd.

The case prior to mine involved thousands of dollars due to injuries and was settled in twenty minutes. At twenty after ten it was "The CITY OF PHOENIX vs. Donald J Litchko.

"Will the attorney for the defense identify himself?" Nobody else moved and I couldn't very well say "no" with all those people looking; so I stood up[and told the Judge that I was going to represent myself. He called me to the bench and whispered that while I was within my legal rights I should realize the self representation is typically not a prudent action.

What could I lose? Ten Dollars! "Thank you your honor I would like to proceed."

The word "objection" took on a whole new meaning that morning and the words "Objection overruled" were not used frequently. In fact they were only used once. In retrospect I now admit that the prosecuting attorney might have had more experience than I.

Question to the first officer; "Did you tell your partner that he did not have to write a ticket in this case?. "OBJECTION, obviously the ticket was issued your honor." He didn't have to shout; all I did was ask a simple question."

I tried to enter pictures of the intersection as evidence, "the defense would like to enter as evidence these pictures showing exactly where the accident occurred; I have but a marker on the street. "OBJECTION; he could have put that marker anywhere on the street." "Your Honor, do I look like the kind of person who would lie to you?" The Judge did not accept the pictures.

To the officer who wrote the ticket; "was this the first ticket you ever wrote?" "OBJECTION, your honor the officer is not on trial here; Mr. Litchko is." By now I was thinking that this guy was trying to intimidate me.

"The defense would like to enter copies of case such and such, which establishes precedence for this case." "OBJECTION your honor; that is a Nevada case and I would like to remind the court that we are in the state of Arizona." Sorry Charlie, experience is no excuse for trying to bluff your way through a trial. "Your Honor the cars were from Nevada, the accident occurred in, and was tried in, Arizona." "Objection overruled." Hey, two can play this game.

There were pictures of the car, sketches on the black board; the calling of the other driver to the stand; descriptions of how the sun was low and perhaps blinding him. And a final question asking; "Why didn't you swerve and try to miss me; there was no other traffic on the street?"

Putting me on the stand and asking me questions brought a little humor to the court room. After two hours even the prosecuting attorney was ready for a smile.

Suddenly the Judge cut it short; "It would appear that you were well through the intersection when you got hit. I find for the defense; not guilty."

I still don't know if I was that good, or, if he was late for a lunch date. I do know that at age twenty-two I learned that the system can and does work. Looking back, the knowledge and experience gained in that two hour court session influenced my life as much as any college course I have ever taken.

Years later I would address Senators and Representatives on various committees in the New Hampshire State House, advocating against unfair health insurance rates issued to the elderly; I, and many others, willing to stand up, and speak up, won the reversal of what we perceived as a discriminating law.

A Bit Of Grandpa Urda

Grandpa Urda was a sitter and a watcher as I remember him. I could best tell when I was pleasing him by his eyes. One evening while hunting woodchucks on the flats up in Smithville I put on an unplanned show that pleased him to no end.

From the front porch Grandpa could look out over the knolls along the road and see most of the tillable acreage on the farm. The flats were nearly a mile long and perhaps a quarter of a mile across. On the far side there was a brush barrier between the hay fields and Genegenslet Creek; a trout stream of local fame.

Milking was done; cows were out and the barn swept clean. My Uncles had gone out on dates and I was alone with my grandparents for the evening. With a piece of homemade bread, covered with apple butter to give me strength, I slipped a few hollow points into my pocket, grabbed the single shot twenty-two from the corner of the closet and went to the knolls to wait for a woodchuck to come out for his evening meal. Grandpa was on the porch, rocking, when I crossed the road.

It was a long shot with open sights and I seldom connected from that range. No dust had kicked up, so there was a chance that I had got him and he fell down in his hole. I couldn't brag about a maybe hit so I hiked across the flats to confirm my kill; once there it was apparent that my aim was consistent with past attempts. I'd get to try for that chuck again. Being now so close to the creek I walked down the tractor trail cutting through the brush to the swimming hole; maybe I could see a trout, and just maybe if I were out of sight for a few minutes that chuck would come back out. Consequently, when I returned to the flats it was with a quiet, cautious approach; every bit like an Indian scout.

I was out in the open just a short way when I caught some movement in the brush off to my left and instinctively froze. From where grandpa was sitting I probably looked like the bronze statue of that soldier standing in the center of Binghamton's Memorial Circle at the junction of the Chenango and Susquehanna rivers.

The doe took a few steps out into the open and eyed me as though she knew I didn't belong there, but didn't know why. Her eyes flickered, and her ears perked up; but the white tail never went up in warning. Slowly and repeatedly she would take a few bites of grass and then stop and give me the once over. I in turn never moved a muscle. A few moments later two smaller deer came out of the brush; possibly her spring fawns. Then some more came out and then even more. Within a few short minutes I had eight deer feeding, walking and playing around me. The smaller ones were like kid's frolicking around in a yard on a summer evening. They would run and tease each other and then stop abruptly, stretch their front legs out so far that their heads would almost touch the ground; and then, as if on a silent signal bounce up and start playing a form of tag. The larger animals continued to eat and mill around, occasionally stopping to give me a quick glance.

I remained frozen with my eyes tearing. I was afraid to even blink; amazed at the situation I found myself in. To this day I believe it happened only because my human scent was covered by the scent of the animals I had milked earlier in the evening; I had not washed or changed clothes after doing chores. Deer often mixed with the cows when they were out to pasture and I am guessing that for this reason they did not spook.

After what seemed to be a half hour one doe came within ten feet of me and entered into a staring contest. She knew I was something wrong and was clever in her attempt to prove it. She would put her head down to the ground to feed and then snap it up quickly to see if she could catch me moving. She would bark to see if the noise would frighten me. (Yes, deer do bark.) Ever so slowly she would raise her hoof and then slap it on a small field stone to see if I could be startled.

Miss Curious was now within four feet of me and I was beginning to get concerned. Those little hoofs were sharp and if she decided to tap on me a bit they could inflict some damage. For whatever reason, fatigue or a little fright, I moved. She jumped back, barked, and raised the white tail in a single action. Poof—they were gone.

Cars had parked up along the road to watch the show; some of them gave me a toot. I started back to the house and it was dark by the time I walked into the kitchen. Normally grandpa would have been in bed; not tonight. He just waited for me and said, "One hour you were out there, one hour."

I remember my grandpa's tough, weathered looking skin and its wrinkles. I remember his yellowed teeth; perhaps from the Druggist Tuck Tobacco we got for him on his birthdays. I remember how he would cough and hack due to the black lung obtained from the years when he worked in the coal mines of Pennsylvania; but most of all I remember his eyes when I walked into the kitchen that night; and I'm glad.

Their Stories

I consider it part of every grandparent's job description to tell stories—and that is a big part of why I am writing this book. Grandma Urda was more inclined to share with me what life was like in Czechoslovakia and we had many, good, one on one visits as I grew up; there were some real advantages to being the oldest grandchild in the family.

On those occasions when Grandpa did tell stories he would just captivate me. He told of what it was like to work in mine tunnels, often not more than three feet tall for hours on end and constantly damp. He told me about the sirens in the mining towns and how when they went off it meant that either there was a cave in, or, almost as bad, that the mules were loose and running mad. He explained how the mules were used to haul the coal carts, always in the dark. Whenever one would break loose and somehow get out into the bright sunlight it would go wild and run through the town trampling gardens, fences, children, and anything else that got in its way. When grandpa got finished I had no doubt that a loose mine mule was something to be feared.

He told me about men dying and having to leave them in their coal dust tombs because of the danger involved with trying to get them out. And he told me about Irish wakes.

Grandpa said that the friction between the Irish and the Solves and Poles was somewhat severe. There was little love lost by either side until disaster struck, and then, for a brief while, they were all just men. Viewings were held in the miner's home and the casket was set up in a corner of the living room as a practical matter; miner's homes were so small that they needed the floor space for the mourners. He also told me that if there was a bottle tucked into the arm of the deceased by the end of the viewing that one could pretty well guess that the friction between the various nationalities would subside for at least a week.

Grandma's stories were many and good. Grandpa's stories were few and great.

• • • • •

School Bus Songs

Riding a school bus eleven miles from Kirkwood to Windsor every morning and returning each afternoon provided time to think, worry about the homework I should have done, and dream about what it would be like if I didn't have to go to school. At least once a week the dreams would be interrupted by school bus songs: "One hundred bottles of beer on the bar, one hundred bottles of beer; take one down and pass it around ninety-nine bottles of beer on the bar; or "so high you can't get over it, so low you can't under it, so wide." When we grew bored with the old standards we would take to modifying the commercials of the day.

"Use AJAX, the foaming cleanser, takes the dirt right down the drain," became "Use AJAX, the foaming toothpaste, takes your teeth right down the drain." And if we really wanted to live on the edge; instead of singing "You'll wonder where the yellow went when brush your teeth with Pepsodent;" we would yell "You'll wonder where the yellow went when you wash your sheets with Pepsodent."

Boom

When you are fourteen, six foot two, and weigh less than a hundred pound and thirty pounds it was only natural that people wonder if my parents were feeding me. They did and did it well. My Mom is a great cook and my Dad was a great provider.

Dad would always have a big garden. The pleasure he derived from planting, hoeing, weeding and harvesting was lost on me until I was on my own and in my late twenties. Gardening was when Dad got some "me" time.

Everything Dad grew Mom canned. Many the night I would be upstairs in bed listening to the pressure cooker go pisst, pisst, pisst, forcing myself to stay awake until I heard one long pissssss as the steam was released and signaled that the process was done and could no longer blow up. Then I knew my mother was safe for another night. Don't know why I was afraid of pressure cookers, but I was.

Canning was not easy work; yet I believe my Mom got more satisfaction out of her career as a house wife than I ever did pushing papers across my desk into some file that might not ever be opened again. In late summer and then every day for the rest of the winter she could see the fruits of her labor on the shelves in the cellar. Quarts of blackberries, pints of wild strawberries sealed with wax. Yellow peaches, white pears with cherries mixed in, orange carrots, deep purple beets sliced like French fries, corn, peas and beans. I enjoyed looking at the shelves. Much more rewarding than writing letters to people

I didn't know, whose faces I would never see and who will never take the time to tell me if they like the contract or not. Mom always knew we liked what she did. The whole family was proud of her shelves.

It occurs to me that stress management classes might do well to include a session or two on canning.

Mom had a reputation as a baker and prided herself on the Hungarian pastries and other sweets she produced each weekend; just in case we had some company. Her reputation was only tainted once; the day she blew all the windows out of the kitchen.

Her stove was fueled from a tall tank of propane which stood upright behind the house. Wooden matches were ignited and dropped through a little hole at the base of the oven in order to light the oven burner. Likewise matches were used to ignite the surface burners. The oven that was thought to have been lit apparently was not; but the gas must have been flowing. When Mom struck a match to one of the top burners; BOOM, swish, tinkle, tinkle, tinkle and all the glass in the windows mingled with the crushed stone in our driveway.

I had been standing near the screen door and after the boom I stumbled or tripped while trying to exit. This all occurred at a time when I couldn't walk and chew gum at the same time. I confess this was a long period in my life; there are days when I'm still a clumsy kid.

A moment of shock, then excitement; "Turn off the burners, turn off the burners." The concern, 'Is everyone all right?" Some tears, "Oh look what I have done." Then I walk back into the kitchen and boom, Mom whacks me a good one, "You didn't have to be so dramatic."

Mom didn't have to get my attention twice. I resolved right then and there that the next time she decided to blow up the house I was going to go down with it. For some reason I never lost another night's sleep over the pressure cooker after that experience.

You Are The Boss

I never gave him credit for always being right; but he was the boss. I will grant that he worked long, hard hours and the company got more than its fair share from him.

"This is a secured facility and when you go home at night everything is to be off your desk." I took it to mean that all correspondence or documentation was to be cleared and locked away. Only the phone, desk calendar and a blank pad of paper were on it when I check out. The next morning I received a lesson in authority in front of the whole office.

"If you don't like following instructions perhaps you would like to go back to the shop floor for the rest of your life. I said everything off and I meant everything off."

He worked late that night and so did I. When I left everything was off my desk including the telephone; I was able to squeeze it into a little side drawer and lock the whole mess up. The cord fit under the little pull out shelf.

Across from the Philadelphia Sales store in Johnson City was a public phone that I never saw anyone use. A dime was deposited; I called myself at work and of course I wasn't there to answer. I let the phone ring and then let the receiver dangle. I then drove home.

I never asked and he never volunteered; but I do believe he went home earlier than he had planned. I do know that when I tried calling my desk from home later that the line was still busy.

No CEO For President

Gatherings with people from work, office parties and the like sometimes made me a bit uncomfortable. Eventually the conversation always touches on work and I feel for the spouses and guests who may not be in tune with the subject at hand.

But such is not always the case—

The matter under discussion was the recent appointment of relatively young Jack Welch as General Electric's CEO; who had recently indicated that if GE was not number one or two in a business we should get out of the that business. Certainly provided some instant incentive for Division Heads to perform.

"Where would he go for satisfaction after heading one of the largest and best managed corporations in the world?" "Perhaps he will run for President."

Pat's husband Joe proved that he was in tune with the corporate world when he immediately replied; "Lord NO; I can see it now—Idaho wasn't number one or two in potatoes last year; Sell IT!

Good Neighbor Policy

If you want good neighbors you have to be a good neighbor. There are times however when the good neighbor policy gets stretched a little.

It was after midnight. I was reading in bed and the rest of the family was asleep. Bang, bang, bang on the back door; "Litchko, I see your light; get your pants on I need help." After letting him in it was obvious that he had been in an accident and equally obvious that he had indulged in one or two. There was dried or frozen blood on his face and his hands had a couple of cuts.

"You have to take me to the hospital."

"Is anything broken? Can you walk?"

"I've been walking for a quarter of a mile. You got to take me."

"Take yourself; you aren't that bad and I need my sleep."

"No, no; I can drive, but they won't believe me. They will think I was drunk."

"Well, they might be right. What won't they believe?"

"That I ran into a bathtub with my snowmobile."

He was a bit tipsy, but he wasn't a liar. He and I had dragged an old cast iron bathtub up to a spring in the woods; intending to dig a hole; sink the tub and put a screen over it; thus would have an ideal spot to keep our minnows for fishing each summer. We just never finished the job.

He had driven the snowmobile over old logging trails to the local American Legion for a short one. On the way home he decided to take a short cut and couldn't see the white tub in the white snow. "A hell of a wreck by any man's account." I agreed; they would never believe him.

I cleaned him up; the cuts were only scratches, and sent him home.

What he needed was warm coffee and a bed. What he got was a cold shoulder and the couch; which proves that the good Lord will only go so far to protect a drunk.

Where Did They Go

Thank goodness that the world of late has been blessed with conscientious individuals who are out to save all of the endangered species and then some. With exception of a few absolute fanatics I applaud a lot of their efforts. I love this world; like someone once said "it's the only planet with chocolate."

I am, however, concerned about one important item which seems to have disappeared without so much as a whisper from mankind. I am highly suspicious that it came to its demise as a result of a conspiracy between the doctor who wrote "you should never put anything in your ear smaller than your elbow," and the manufacturer of cotton swabs. Tell me. What has become of Bobbie pins and why are we taking their passing so lightly.

Remember Bobbie pins, those wires your mother would stick in her hair? There were two basic kinds. My Grandma Urda used the long kind that were made of round wire and had crinkles up near the "U" part. Sometimes she bought white ones so that they wouldn't show; grandma had snow white hair. I never liked that type much because they were like electrical wire, flexible and soft.

My mother used the other kind; the ones that were made from flattened, tempered wire. She would buy fifty or so that were sticking through a long slot on a cardboard card. They were always near the checkout counter of the grocery store along with the razor blades and like. The flat ones were best because you could always bend one side back and twang it to make a sound like a Jews harp. You could also, and I often did, wad up that piece of tin foil that was around every stick of gum; form it into a "V;" put it on the bent and springy hairpin and send it across a class room. No longer a hair pin; it was a miniature catapult. Mrs. Turrell was up front talking about history and I was in the back of the room reliving it; until I got caught; and then we were both up front.

Sometimes when I got nervous my Dad would yell "stop biting your nails;" so instead I would take mom's Bobbie pins and pull off the little nubs of whatever it was that they put on the ends of Bobbie pins so that women would not accidently stab themselves. Then on Saturday mornings when it was my turn to vacuum I could hear those same little things going ping, ping, as they were sucked up the metal tube of the Electrolux.

But best of all, and what I missed the most, is that you could use them to clean your ears. None of this insert the cotton ball and gently twirl stuff. With a Bobbie pin you could go in and scrape, get right to those itchy spots. Then you could clean it off by squeezing it between your thumb and forefinger. You could smell the wax on your fingers until the next time you washed; and that was okay because it was a part of you.

Save the crocodiles, elephants and rain forest; that's all fine and good; but, let us not forget the Bobbie pin.

Stress Management

Among all of the self perpetuating activities Stress Management Courses must rank near the top. I have attended several; each sponsored by someone in higher management trying to resolve a guilt complex. Deep down they know they are asking too much of you but keep piling on the work so that they can be competitive. "Let's get an expert to help them cope." It is nice that they are so concerned.

The first thing I noticed about Stress Management classes is that there will always be some major panic, some occurrence that requires one hundred and ten percent of my time on the day of the course. Schedule it on a Sunday and I'd bet a paycheck that some airline would call me at home an hour before the class with a message that they have an airplane on the ground for lack of one of our parts.

The second thing you can count on is that nobody will be assigned to do my job while I am at the stress management class; which perpetuates, you guessed it—STRESS.

The third thing you can count on is that 99 % of the things you learn consist of things you need to do on your own time. "What you should do is make time for yourself—do some exercises—take an hour hike; you deserve it, you have worked a long, hard day. Relax." The people who thought this up obviously did not leave a wife with three kids at home for ten or twelve hours while you worked; that same wife who just can't wait for you to step through the door to give her a little stress relief. Imagine her joy when if I would announce that from now on I want an hour to myself every night before supper.

In no particular order let me relate some of the wisdom gained in some of these courses: Touching is a form of stress relief; it is a way of expressing feeling and concern. A good sex life can be a form of stress relief.

Would you believe that the same manager who hired this dispenser of wisdom two weeks later sent me to another class on sexual harassment in which the message was "hands off."

Then she told us to get rid of our aggressive feelings. She actually armed us with soft rubber bats and encouraged us to club each other. "Now don't you feel better?"

"Hell yes," but the first time I tried to get one of my customers to pick up the rubber bat during a negotiation he suggested that maybe I needed a rubber walled room.

"Make quality time for yourself," she said with a slow, soft voice; while I was wishing she would shut up so that I could get home to my kids birthday party,

One firm I worked for in Texas actually took to heart all this stuff about exercise and purchased all sorts of mats, weights, stationary bikes and muscle building equipment; even hired a physical education instructor to urge us on. When the business almost failed a year later for lack of funds they laid off three hundred of the three hundred and thirty people that worked for them. That was so stress relieving I didn't work for four months.

So what is the answer? How do we break the stress cycle? Here are some of Litch's recommendations; free advice just waiting to be acted upon.

Start by allowing me to work eight hours of flex time each month so that when I walk in the door and my six year old runs up and says "Daddy can you come to my school play; I'm going to be a tree" I can say yes and mean it, right on the spot. Or maybe I could go fishing on a Friday afternoon before the cold front moves in, and work indoors on Saturday when it is raining.

Declare one day a month "Blue Jeans and NO Meeting Day." Just being able to dig in and find the bottom of my desk once a month would relieve a lot of stress.

Instead of spending thousands for company picnics, dances and parties that I then feel obligated to attend on my own time; surprise me with free tickets so I can take my kids to a ball game, or my wife to a play.

Give a good mechanic some garage space on company property so that he could do my car inspections and change my oil while I'm at work without having to arrange for rides or tying to cram them in on a Saturday morning.

But the best idea—the best bang for the buck—is so simple. Once a week say "thanks" even if the results weren't perfect. At least acknowledge that I gave it one hell of a try. That would relive a lot of stress.

Is They Is Or Is They Not

I find compliments to be among the most confusing and difficult things to cope with in life. When I do something well, darned if I don't think I deserve one; then when I get one, darned if I don't feel embarrassed about receiving it. Sometimes compliments can be confusing because of the way they are delivered.

The early morning flight was in the midst of the Seattle rush hour. The three of us had a hard time getting started and got up late; then to make matters worse the checkout line at the Red Lion was uncharacteristically long.

I drove over curbs and through yellow lights so close to being red that they were pink. I made it from the breakdown lane across four lanes of traffic and back at least twice. Fellow drivers in Seattle were giving me hand signs that made me think I was driving in the Bronx.

Twelve minutes after getting behind the wheel we were at the departure curb at SEATAC; a remarkable feat on any morning in Seattle. My passengers were quiet throughout the brief trip; but when former astronaut Bill Anders stepped out of the car he did mention something about "and I thought going to the moon was exciting."

I think it was a compliment; he was a very results oriented person and I did get him to his flight on time; but have noted that he never rode with me again.

Come Fly With Me

Flying at the expense of others has been one of the perks I have enjoyed throughout most of my career. Sure the frequent flyer miles were nice, but that was not the best part. Hearing and feeling engines so relatively small drag a 747, or 757 down a runway and then pull all of that weight up into the sky to cruise at six hundred miles an hour just thrills me.

My first flight was in a flying box car, compliments of the Civil Air Patrol. My dad was a furniture salesman at Olum's in Johnson City. Taking me to Mount Erick, now known as Link Field, meant he had to get up early and drive an extra twenty five miles just so I could have an adventure; Dad was always good that way. That first flight was exciting; sitting in a low slung, webbed seat, bent over due to having to wear a parachute pulled tight from my shoulders to my crotch with the rip cord dangling right where it should be. I think I might have weighed all of a hundred and ten pounds at the time; just a tall thin kid; but I felt like I was John Wayne. My back was against the fuselage so that I felt every vibration so acute that after a short time I knew when the propos were being trimmed just by the feel of the plane. I marveled that the plane could taxi with just one prop. Looking up at the line we were to snap our rip cords on in case an emergency jump was necessary I remember feeling like "man I was just something."

Today's jets taxi to the end of the runway and zoom; off you go. When I was fourteen, on a prop plane, that's not the way it happened. The pilot taxied to the end of the run way and aligned for takeoff. He would then plant the wheel brakes firm and rev up one engine until you thought it would fly apart. That roar would subside as he throttled back prior to repeating the process with the other engine. Control surfaces were checked, flaps up and down, rudder back and forth, and then quiet while he waited for clearance from the tower. There was anticipation, a suspense that built up during that quiet time that made your insides want to explode.

Let's do it.

Part of the thrill of riding in a military craft was that you could look directly into the cockpit and hear the conversation between the pilot and the tower. The words "cleared for takeoff" just added to the excitement. Power was applied to one engine and then the other, props were trimmed to keep both in sync and the whole plane stood still and just shuddered; begging for the brakes to be released.

There was absolutely no fear on that (my) first flight. It was all thrill and amassment. Some of the guy's chatted excitedly, others tried to shout over the din. Flying boxcars had not been designed for quiet or passenger comfort. For my part I just sat quiet and when CAP Lt. Teddy Mulcahy walked by and asked how I was doing all she got was a smile and thumbs up; for once in my life I was indeed quiet. It was a one and a half hour orientation flight. My joy of having been on it must have shown because when the pilot exited the plane he walked over and said he needed a copilot for the next flight after lunch and wondered if I would like the job.

Was he kidding; "Well I do have a copilot but we have an extra seat up front if you want to go back up." Wow; double wow! He didn't have to ask twice. I ran through the airport to call my Dad and tell him not to worry if I wasn't on the ground when he came to pick me up. I don't recall asking him if it would be okay. My dad was very understanding about such things.

This time I was the first one on the plane and took the seat nearest the cockpit. I had flown before you know, and was now experienced. Once up and leveled off the copilot came back to give a brief lecture to the cadets; as he walked by he motioned for me to take his seat.

When I had left the house that morning who would have ever thought that on that same day I would be at the controls of a plane? My feet on the pedals, my hands on the yoke, earphones on, looking at compasses, artificial horizons, air speed indicators, altimeters and a whole bunch of other instruments.

It was a banner day. I didn't just fly; I flew. I really flew an airplane (however briefly) my first time up.

Perhaps it was to become a hereditary thing because about thirty years later my daughter Laura flew a plane her first time up; but that is her story to tell.

There was no way of knowing at the time that I would later spend nearly forty years of my life working in the aerospace industry; building flight and weapon control systems, managing instrument development programs; meeting an astronaut; and even having to pull off of I-93 north of Boston once to take an emergency call concerning the Presidents helicopter. (It was a good call because while there was a problem; it had nothing to do with the firm I worked for.)

The Excitement Never Stopped

Occasionally a flight provides some extra excitement and some interesting observations. The small twin engine plane only held four passengers and we were in rather tight quarters as we left Link Field for Dulles International; where I was to catch a flight to Seattle. I was in the back and the guy next to me was reading a Playboy. I tried desperately just to look out the window but am reasonably certain that was what he was reading. Someplace over Pennsylvania, near Montrose, one prop just stopped. No slow down, no flutter; it just stopped.

The pilot immediately radioed the tower in Binghamton and stated we had lost an engine and were returning to the airport; as we were only fifteen or twenty minutes out. The plane never lost altitude and had I been napping would never had known there was a problem. Once square with the tower the pilot turned and told us not to worry; "we could fly all day with just one engine." We believed him; at least until it came time to land.

"Cessna Bravo, bravo, one, one niner this is the tower."

"Tower, this is Cessna Bravo, bravo, one, one niner; go ahead.

"Ah Charile; look, according to FAA regulations we are required to have emergency equipment on ready standby as you come in. Do you want them on standby in the hanger or do you want them on standby along the runway?"

"Bill; I think for this one they better be on the runway."

I'm not sure what faith, if any, the other three passengers had; but do believe I witnessed two conversions.

WHAT A CHARGE

Got hit with lightening once and found it to be a neat experience—once—once my nerves settled down. We were flying at about twenty thousand feet; passing through clouds with only a bit of turbulence; not a rough flight at all. Occasionally there would be a flash and it would appear through the clouds as a dull light; something like you might see at an amateur theater production. Suddenly everything around the plane lit up so bright it hurt my eyes.

The engines never stopped. The interior lights never flickered. The neat part, however, was the force. For ever so brief a moment we all plunged forward in our seats. It was that same feeling as when you got caught running in the halls in grade school and some teacher grabbed you by the shoulders in mid stride and said "woooooo there, lets slow it down a bit." Same kind of feeling you had as a kid when some fat aunt held you whiling trying to give you a kiss. You just got shoved ahead, with no chance to resist; and once it was over you were just happy to get away and be able to breathe again.

Upon landing I noticed the nose of the plane had a burn mark on it; and I walked away with a whole new appreciation for the people who designed aircraft structures and electrical systems. And then I tipped my hat to the flight crew that took one on the nose and still had nerve enough to provide us with a safe landing.

Butt Out

Unlike today there was a time when you were allowed to smoke on planes.

I recall hearing about us crossing some special mountain and as usual it was on the opposite side of the plane from where I was sitting. On a 747 you can't very well say excuse me, excuse me, excuse me a dozen times just to look out the other window so I went back to sleep. Next thing I remember was waking up and looking down on the passenger to my left. The jumbo plane was banking like it was a fighter, not a transport. I looked at my travel companion and said, "If I didn't know better I'd say we have just been high jacked and are headed to Canada." Unsaid was my fear that that we might be headed over the North Pole to Russia; I sometime have a flare for the dramatic. On the other hand this happened when plane high jacking was the rage. Sky marshals were just beginning to be added to some flights and metal detectors were just beginning to appear at some of the major airports.

The pilot alleviated our concerns when he announced that one passenger had refused to put out his cigar; and that his management had directed him to put the plane down at the nearest airport; "we are headed to Fargo, North Dakota where the runways are long enough to accommodate this aircraft." After a few moans and groans about the delay there was relative peace and tranquility; that is until it was time to land.

Instead of "Return your seats to the upright position," we were instructed to bend over and assume the crash position and remain that way even after landing. The Captain was adamant that we not get up or move "NO MATTER WHAT happens."

Upon a very normal landing the plane was surrounded by men I presumed to be Marshalls and plain clothes men. The hundreds of people on board remained calm with heads down as instructed. A short marshal boarded and moments later I saw him pushing a tall guy down the aisle. The big guy was saying something like "this just isn't like me, I've never done anything like this before." The Marshall told him to "Move it you a—h—."

The incident made national news that evening and undoubtedly was passed off by most as one of those things that happens to someone else; but I remember:

One Northwest Airline crew that had the wisdom to think that if one guy would not put a cigar out that maybe he was capable of doing much worse; and that on the ground one airline stood behind their pilot and supported his decision despite the tremendous cost associated with landing, refueling, and putting a 747 back into the air.

I remember all of the passengers giving the crew a loud ovation for taking the action; and I remember telling my kids, while watching television that evening, that I was there.

DISPENSING MOTIVATION

Dispensing discipline in the work place can be a necessary and somewhat painful task, or, a creative experience; it depends on the attitude of the dispenser.

It was necessary that the gyroscopes being designed for the new F-18 fighter pass a lengthy vibration and temperature test sequence known to the designers as the shake and bake test. The units literally had to run failure free for days on end. The schedule was critical and each morning I would get up at three-thirty and drive to the plant to check on the results of the ongoing test. In the event of any failure I wanted to have a plan in place by the time the design team arrived at eight o'clock.

The first morning, unannounced, I walked into the test area; found the test chamber and gyros working perfectly and the technician, who should have been monitoring the test—sound asleep.

I thought I was most professional in the way I woke him and explained the importance of his job. I admitted that I knew it was boring, particularly when there were no failures, and suggested he not fall asleep again.

The next morning I found him asleep in the same chair. My dissertation was not nearly as professional; we paid him to stay awake. I hated to document the incident; by all accounts he was a talented young engineer and the company had high hopes for him in the future.

When I awoke the third morning there was a stirring in the crib next to our bed and I changed a diaper prior to hitting the road. I walked into the test area on my tip toes and the sound of a soft snore did not disappoint me.

Black chinos were the in thing that year; this was just before the polyester leisure suit craze.

While he slumbered I sprinkled Johnson and Johnson's baby powder on the black chinos in an area roughly one hundred and eighty degree opposite his bottom. I quietly left; and then made a noisy reentry; and acted pleased to find him standing by the test stand. "What's that?" I asked pointing to his crotch. He immediately started brushing the powder and in the process rubbed it deeper and deeper into the black fabric.

It was pure joy watching that young man trying to hide and inconspicuously leave the plant. Never again did he sleep on the job; nor was there ever a blemish on his record and in years later he truly did some great things for the firm.

Truth may come from the mouths of babes; justice however came that morning from a baby's bottom. Thank you, Laura.

Sometimes I'm Sorry

Phone calls at midnight were not common at our house and when Mr. Philley, the high school principal, started to ask if I was home, the phone was left dangling as my Dad charged into my bed and was relieved to find me there.

"Mr. Litchko why I am calling is that a man outside the village went out hunting this afternoon and he hasn't returned yet. I have been asked to round up some boys to help with a search." I was dressed and ready to start hiking in a flash. There were police cars galore around the old Occanum Restaurant; newspaper and radio personnel were there as well.

The State Troopers arranged us in single file. We climbed the mountain and spread out such that you could always see and hear the person in front and in back of you. Once the point man reached the top we started to hike across the face of the hill. Take twenty paces, stoop, yell, and listen. Take twenty more spaces, stop, yell and listen. Various teams canvassed selected sections and once your section was done you hiked down the hill and back to base; that first morning things were not organized enough to have pick-up trucks waiting for us.

To say that we conducted the search in mountains is a slight exaggeration. Windsor is located in the foothills of the Catskills, on the west side of the range. The hills around Windsor can be steep. The zone I was assigned to ran from twelve hundred feet to nineteen hundred feet in short order; some of the highest points in Broome County. By noon the first day I had been part of four sweeps. When a reporter asked if I thought the hill had been covered I told him I thought I had covered it myself.

By the second day dogs and professional man hunters were brought in to assist in the effort. We had no clue as to the man's whereabouts. He was known to be asthmatic, carrying a shotgun, and hunting without a dog. There was speculation that he may have hiked to Route 17, caught a ride, and skipped town; though nobody could offer the slightest reason why he might have done so. There was a nagging question as to why a man with a gun would not have fired shots to signal if he needed help. There were trips and trips and trips across the hill.

On the third day I sat resting on a boulder near the top, looking down on the Susquehanna River when an older gentleman, maybe in his fifties, came up. We exchanged pleasantries and shortly I did some mild complaining about how tough it was to make the repeated trips. He agreed it was tiring; "Especially since my accident; I only have one lung."

He was one of the professionals the State Police had called in to help. On our why back to base he taught me to look up into the trees as well as under windfalls and on the ground. He told me of once finding a guy thirty feet up in a tree that he had walked under a dozen times during a particular search. Claimed the guy had fallen over the edge of a cliff right next to where the search party had set up their base camp. Nobody had thought to look up.

After many continuous days and many subsequent volunteer weekends the search was abandoned. With so many searchers, and so many searches, it was presumed the guy had skipped town.

Some years later his bones, boots, and rusty gun were found across the creek in the middle of a blackberry patch. He had hunted on easy, relatively flat ground.

The local boys and men had been assigned to the hills and mountains. Out of town folks who didn't know the area were assigned to the pastures and open fields; and they probably figured nobody would walk though all those briers.

From time to time I wonder if a local guy with some hunting savvy might not have walked right through that blackberry patch knowing that a man hunting without a dog would have to kick out his own bunnies.

Sometimes to this day, I think about it and I'm sorry.

Don't Stick It

Everyone has a favorite something or other; some have several favorite somethings or others; for instance pencils. I have a couple that I like, they just feel comfortable in my hand; both are modern .05 lead jobs with those tiny, almost delicate, erasers that are hid under shinny metal caps. Perhaps that is the reason I like them so much. Truth is I have developed a phobia about mechanical pencils with large erasers on top. I even remember when and where the fear developed.

I was in Utica, New York, in a building on French Road sitting near the middle of a large conference table. The group consisted of very important individuals that thought that they were very important individuals. They were gathered to solve some ills in this particular corporate world. I had never met any of them prior to this meeting; and was suitably impressed with their titles, and was almost in awe just to be in their midst.

The chairperson had said his piece and a couple of others had offered comments when deep inside my right ear I developed an awful itch; possibly some shaving cream had got in there and dried out during the drive from Binghamton. I tried laying my hand alongside my head in a meaningful pose at the same time sticking my index finger in to get some relief; to no avail. I tried moving my jaw into funny positions when I thought nobody was looking but the itch remained; if anything it got worse. I had to do something; the sensation was so bad I couldn't concentrate on the serious subject at hand.

In desperation I took the mechanical pencil out of my inner coat pocket and proceeded to shove the eraser end into my ear; cranking it as I went. I pulled it off without anyone noticing and was blessed with almost immediate relief; unfortunately I was also blessed with immediate deafness. I extracted the pencil alright, but the eraser had lodged inside my ear. I couldn't hear a damn thing anyone was saying on my right side.

I smiled and tried to nod my head at the right time; but after getting a couple of funny looks for turning left and right when I should have nodded up and down, I found it prudent to excuse myself and head for the privacy of the nearest men's room.

I was alone, staring at the mirror and absolutely unable to reach the eraser with my finger. Still a Boy Scout at age thirty-seven I pulled out my jackknife, open the pointed blade and prepared to stab the rubber plug, when a guy walks in, takes one look and shouts, "Oh God NO."

I think he must have participated in some of the executive conferences at French Road. I speared the eraser; and he laughed when I revived him. And I made it a habit to always carry a jackknife until the airlines started to collect them at the security check points; after donating four in two months it just became cost prohibitive.

AIN'T NECESSARILY SO

I lived with the widow next door for several months, once, and remember it fondly. Bertie Thompson had a teenage son, a limited income and a room to rent. I was living away from home for the first time and found that when my roommate was placed on second shift it strained our relationship. He needed to sleep when I wanted to make noise. When he came strolling into our one room efficiency at two in the morning and started to rattle a few pans while preparing a snack; I was not my gentle, patient self. I jumped fence and took the room Bertie had for rent next door.

Bertie was a good Christian woman trying to raise a young son. I offered to leave my small collection of amber fluids with friend Marty if she so desired. I wanted to send the signal that I would respect her rules, in her house, right from the start. Bertie told me that while she would not hold to any serious drinking it would be okay if I kept my small collection in my room. She went on to say that every now and then she enjoyed a little glass of wine.

The deal was cut. For a set fee I had a room, breakfast, supper, and she would iron five dress shirts each week. I moved in.

One look at that first supper table and I wanted to laugh; it was obvious that Bertie had gone out of her way to put me at ease on the drinking matter. Set near each plate was a goblet of wine so large that the Pope could have given communion to the multitudes and still had some left over. Bertie didn't drink often and it was a bit obvious that she sure didn't have any idea when enough was enough.

She was a small thin woman and in her soft Texas voice she said, "Don, now Jim and I would be most appreciative if you would be so kind as to say grace."

"Certainly;" my voice started with "Bless us, O Lord, and these thy gifts," while my mind was praying, "good Lord, how am I going to get that much wine down without offending her at our first meal.

Grace finished, I raise my goblet and made a brief toast; much to their surprise. The glass touched my lips; I tipped it up and proceeded to stick my nose into the biggest glob of grape Jell-O I had ever seen.

My mother never made grape Jell-O; we always had the red kind.

Only Enough To Stick

As long as I lived in the Thompson house and as much a Bertie treated me like family, only once could I accuse her of interfering with my lifestyle.

On a Saturday morning, two weeks before Christmas she knocked on my bedroom door at six in the morning and ordered me up. "Don, I need your help today, now go take a shower." Bertie was tiny and somewhat frail in appearance, but I wasn't about to offer any debate when she spoke in that tone. As I was drying off she stood around the corner and told me that there was a clean pair of jeans on my bed and that I was to put them on. "Don't worry about a shirt and come into the kitchen; quickly please." If her son Jim had not clued me in a couple of weeks earlier I would have been concerned. Even though forewarned I was not prepared for the transformation that had taken place in her little kitchen.

On the table was buckets of pecans all shelled and ready to eat; full gallon containers of candied cherries, pineapples and too many other fruits to identify; some new to me; they were all there and in abundance. On the floor was a big galvanized wash tub; the very same kind that my grandma would give me a bath in when I was a little guy. All over the counters were bread pans stacked criss-crossed, like firewood. Out in the TV room I could see cooling racks in every conceivable location.

I grew up in the north where Christmas delicacies consisted of kolachi, poppy seed rolls and similar goodies prevalent to the nationality of the home you were visiting. Bertie was from the South and in her home Christmas was fruitcake; and I was about to learn the art.

Down on my knees, stripped to my waist; a kerchief wrapped around my head; not for sweat, but because "nobody is going to find a hair in my fruitcake, young man." I trust they never did. I was the human mixmaster as Bertie and Jim dumped gallon after gallon of sticky fruit of every imaginable color into the tub. The fun of it all quickly turned to work as the mixture rose over my elbows. Hand mixing mortar for my Dad when he was laying cinderblocks was easier by a long shot. The fruit was not only sticky, it was heavy; and this was work.

While I mixed the fruit Bertie made batter and Jim licked spoons. The electric mixer she used did not have to work nearly as long as I did because "in a good fruit cake you only put in enough batter to hold the fruit together." The less batter the better the cake; and Bertie's cakes were excellent.

Once the whole concoction was blended together I was sent back to the shower; this time to see if hot water could somehow help get my fingers apart. I was content just to let the hot water pound on my shoulders. Two hours of fruitcake mixing was equivalent to tossing bales on the farm for a whole day.

I returned into the kitchen in time to watch Bertie pour and soak each hot cake with rum—the kitchen filled with a mild steam; and then the pans were set to cool.

I was raised in a family that cherished tradition at the holidays. Christmas Eve supper consisted of foods that were not prepared at any other time of the year; Midnight Mass and large family gatherings on Christmas day were the norm. I never knew anything else and admit to being homesick that first Christmas away from home. Three people sitting at a table eating ham hocks and brown eyed peas was not the same as sitting at my parents table; with its platters of rich pastries, bowls of dried mushroom soup, warm milk and honey with poppy seeds. Fish, shrimp and fresh breads surrounded by people who knew you well and loved you.

Yet, now, looking back, I think this was perhaps my Christmas of most importance.

I was raised to be color blind and put downs due to ones nationality were not long tolerated in the house I grew up in. That first Christmas away from home, somehow brought all of those values into focus. It was something a little deeper than just words and the example my parents had passed on. Ham hocks were as special to Bertie and Jim as my grandma's pastries were to me. Making enough fruit cakes to share with the whole world (we had made thirty or forty cakes) was in Bertie's way the same as our having the all the family in for dinner on Christmas day.

Most important from that first Christmas away from home was that I realized that my parents were not alone in their values. There are lots of families and homes with open doors, and kitchen tables set with coffee cups and a little wine; ready to be shared with a friend. Each family's traditions may be a little different, but the values are all the same.

I learned my lesson well so when you come to our home, please don't be afraid to open the fridge and help yourself, if you are so inclined. And if you are more comfortable walking barefoot; don't ask, just take those shoes off.

And please don't mind me if I'm a little overbearing when I urge you to relax and enjoy; you see, I still remember how nice I was treated my first Christmas away from home.

SURE MR. LITCHKO

The streets of Tokyo in the Ginza were wall to wall people in the afternoon and then, at night, they got crowded. At two in the morning, upon exiting the club where my host had made more than enough Crown Royal available, I asked, "Sato San, are the streets of Tokyo ever empty?" With a laugh and a slap on the shoulder he said "Sure Mr. Litchko; when American bombers come over."

He and I could never have laughed this way the year I was born.

I include this story for the benefit of those who seem to think thinks are so bad in the world that they just can't be changed. Thirty-five years after the big war and one generation later I had a friend in Japan.

You Want Equility You Got It

When equal rights legislation was finally put in place it didn't take long for the rumblings of reverse discrimination to start sweeping through the plant. Employment was stable and new hires were minimal. The competition for in-house promotions was keen. I found it ironic that the ones least qualified were the ones most concerned about this alleged to be unfair treatment in favor of minorities.

I was seasoned enough to know there were probably only one or two voice boxes and a whole bunch of head nodders. Head nodders are people smart enough to know it makes no sense to argue with a voice box; so they just keep their mouths shut and just nod. Unfortunately the voice boxes all believed the head nodders were in total agreement with them and thus claimed "everybody feels this way."

It took me three weeks to sniff out Ms. Voice Box; she had recently applied for a position as group leader.

She was wearing a sleeveless blouse; sitting at her work station when I walked up; "Hi, Mr. Litchko." We exchanged some small talk as I watched her work; then I took out an extra wide felt tip pen. Starting at her shoulder I drew a black line down to her elbow. She felt it but could not see the mark the first time. "What are you doing?" She sort of giggled as I drew the next line—somewhat of a nervous giggle it was. "Oh I just want to assure that you will be looked at like all other applicants when I select the new group leader." There was no reply and her face got as red as the black pen was black. I did catch a few smiles and snickers as I walked away.

Today I probably would have been fired. In some parts of the country there were whites who would have killed me; maybe yet, but not likely in Johnson City, New York.

After that in Litchko's department talk about discrimination may have been whispered; but only in extreme private; because "you just never know what that old bastard might do."

• • • • •

Here Comes The Judge

Was sitting in a family card game at Madeline and Neil Griffin's kitchen table one evening when an excited neighbor came through the door. Her concern was that there was going to be a town election and there had not been a two party town board in past thirty years. "Worse than that, we can't get anyone to run." She was right; everyone knew that in Kirkwood the real election took place in the primaries.

Always a sucker for a good cause and having registered as a member of the opposition, I casually asked "what seats are up this year?" "Well there is the tax collector; but what we really need is someone to run for Town Justice; because the JP not only dispenses justice, but he also sits on the town board.

I was holding a full house and took it as a good sign. "Hey, I don't know anything about politics, but if you really need someone you can throw my name in the hat; "Here comes the Judge." I lost that hand to the only four of a kind all night; should have told me something but I didn't notice.

I jumped a few minor hurdles that first week. In order to run I had to be a landowner. I wasn't, so my mom and dad quickly sold me one landlocked acre in the middle of their property for a dollar. A sympathetic lawyer filed a quick deed the next day for no charge. Months later I sold the lot back to them.

In order to run I had to register with the board of elections, which meant I had to decide who to run against. One JP was a member of our church and the other was a next door neighbor.

There was an official party caucus of some sort and the five of us decided I was running.

I had a thirty year jump on those who wanted to curtail campaign spending. My war chest consisted of $98.00 and any extra gas money Carole and I could scuff up each week; we spent it wisely. Paid the County three dollars for all of the Kirkwood tax maps; bough a new suit and some imitation wing tips; and then bought a hat; at twenty-seven felt I needed something to make me look older. Took the seventeen dollars I had left and bought some business cards and a five dollar ad in the local "Pennysaver."

The tax maps were taped to my garage wall, now my new campaign headquarters. Proceeded to map out a timetable to visit every single home in the town of Kirkwood and three months later I think knew more and had seen more, and cared more for the town of Kirkwood than the town historian.

One old lady told me the last time a politician knocked on her door he was giving away nickel candy bars; I gave her my card. One family was living in a tent; year around. They were surprised I made it around the dog; "not many do; kinda a waste of time for ya because we don't vote." One beautiful house had an immaculate lawn, wrought iron lawn furniture; and dirt floors inside. I don't mean dirty floors, I mean dirt floors—I'll never forget it.

Some people slammed doors in my face. "Hello, I'm Don Litchko and I'm running for—," "We know who you are?" BOOM. The wind from the door would knock my hat off.

One polite lady explained that her husband was the Town Supervisor and she hoped that I would understand if I didn't get her vote; I should have done my home work. Another chastised me for being so cruel; referring to my opponent, "Why he only needs two more terms to get his retirement."

Sarah, the eighty year old town clerk gave me a ten dollar campaign donation; said it was worth it just to see those guys squirm. I think she wanted to cover her bets in case by some quirk I won. She had learned a lot in eighty years.

One prominent citizen, a member of the other party, offered to deliver votes for a small nominal fee. I was so green and she was so smooth that I was four doors down the street before I realize I had just been propositioned.

Sometime I was conned into making mistakes. On one street, for three homes in a row I gave my "hello, I'm Don Litchko" introduction and each homeowner laughed and said "You know who I thought you were? I thought you were a Jehovah Witness." A block away she opened the door and said, "you know who I thought you were?' I laughed, interrupted her and said "yes, you thought I was a Jehovah Witness."

I wasn't, but she was. On election night when I lost by just sixty some votes I wondered for a long time if there were sixty Jehovah Witnesses in the town of Kirkwood.

If everybody who came up to me the following week and said "If I thought you were going to get that close I would have gone down and voted," had indeed voted for me—I would have won.

In fact I did win. I learned that small town politics can be tough. I learned that no matter how hard you try some people will always take it out of context. And I learned that with help from a lot of people one person can make a difference.

Based on my almost success another young man, Joe Griffin, ran for town supervisor the following year and won. I believe the Town of Kirkwood has had a two party board ever since.

I got to know a delightful eighty year old town Clerk who had the scoop on everyone, and a young lady named Suzie that I still believe could run for President. I met a donkey that smoked cigarettes. And I almost got to say "Here comes the judge; here comes the judge."

Not Fast

I was out almost as soon as I left first base. I slowed to a walk the instant I knew the second baseman had the ball. His teammates were headed to the dugout even before he made the tag.

Couch Howard called me over, put his hands on my shoulders and pulled me down so he could look me right in the eyes. "Litchko, when you decide to steal a base there are two things I want you to remember; FIRST you are not fast and SECOND, once you decide to go NEVER stop."

The score was tied; I got a blooper into right field. The first base coach kept saying "stay put, stay put."

My mind kept saying "after that last time they won't be looking for it; if you get the chance, go." The next pitch was in the dirt and I took off. For certain Coach Howard was saying "Litchkooooooooooo" as he threw his hat in the dirt. All I heard was something inside my head saying "don't stop, don't stop." Brian Sheehy caught the throw and was waiting; waiting for me to slow down; waiting directly between second base and me. "Never stop, never stop." Old never stop Litchko dove headfirst for second base.

Brian's leg broke clean as I remember, but it must have hurt like hell because he dropped the ball. I took second and third.

The game ended in a tie because without Brian and the four guys who carried him to the nurse's office the other team was short handed. I truly felt bad that I had broken his leg; and later felt even worse when I remembered that report cards were coming out in two weeks and his father was my English teacher.

Coach Howard's advice however was a real gift. My only disappointments in life have occurred when for some reason I slowed down after having made a decision to "go."

No Coincidence

Eliminate the word Coincidence from your vocabulary and life becomes instantaneously exciting; suddenly every happening begs the question "Why." Wait long enough and the whys get answered.

My Dad came home from his gas station for lunch one day just in time to hear an old lady on Ronan Street swearing at me, his three year old, in Polish, because I had picked a couple of her flowers. "Nobody should swear at a child;" and an almost immediate decision was made to move his family out of Binghamton and into the country where kids could have enough land to run, jump, pick climb and do whatever kids were meant to do, without having some old battle-ax curse at them. He acted on that decision by buying the old Murphy farm on Trim Street, in Kirkwood. That farm, for what it was, and what my parents turned it into, is what I called home. As a kid I did indeed run, climb and even pick on those hundred plus acres without any encumbrances. (Years later Father Murphy, a most pleasant and popular Priest was assigned to Our Lady of Lourdes Parish in Windsor; during one conversation we discovered that as boys we had both slept in the same bedroom; and he knew about the "Indian chair" tree up in the woods.)

The farm included a stand of hardwoods, red oaks; and many approached nearly thirty six inches diameter at the stump level. They were giant tress of great beauty and old age. Dad loved the woods and even though his job as a salesman at Olum's furniture store required him to be on his feet five and six days a week, every Sunday he would take a walk around his woods with at least one or two of us kids in tow.

On my journeys with Dad I typically picked up a walking stick which became a balancing beam when I climbed, and walked along the tops of old stone walls; or a vaulting pole when I jumped over fallen trees. It became a spear when I was an Indian and a rifle when I was a cowboy. Sometimes the stick became a real necessity in order to whack my way through underbrush, briers and other vegetation; all of which I pretended was a bunch of bad guys. Dad would let me do my thing until we got to the oaks and then, without fail he would say; "Donnie, don't hit these trees, these are Boze's (God's) trees.

The years pass; I grow older, as do the trees. Married with two children of my own it is time to build a house. Build is the operative word here. Due to finances at the time it was "to build" not "to have built" a house. I was to be the carpenter, plumber and electrician. Mom and Dad were anxious to help and called me aside one day; "Don, it is time to cut the trees; take what timber you need to build the house." These were high inflation years and the cost of lumber was dear. Between the financial benefit and knowing my Dad's love for his trees, this was no insignificant gift.

About twenty of the huge oaks were felled, trimmed out, cut into logs, dragged out and then stacked on skids to await pickup for a trip to the mill.

The house was built the following year; however, due to a financialy attractive package deal from Whipples Lumber the oaks were never used; they remained on skids up on the hill.

Another year passed. Friends visit and my love for wood shows as I brag a bit about the solid cherry cupboards I fashioned in the kitchen. One day at work, Bill, one of those friends stops at my desk.

"Litch, you doing anything next Tuesday night?"

"You want to play poker on a week night?"

"No, no, but I'll tell you what. Our church, (Saint Andrews on Conklin Ave) has had a new crucifix carved for behind the alter; it is a large piece and different. The nun who carved it sees things differently; and is interesting. She is going to give a talk to some of us before the formal dedication. I know you and your brother like wood and stuff and I thought maybe you would like to sit in and hear her on Tuesday night. It's your kind of thing."

My brother Dick and I slipped into the back of the meeting room; strangers to all present except Bill, who had invited us. Bill had no knowledge of the oak logs up on the hill. Sister Paula was introduced. Bill was right, she did have, and shared, different feelings and the crucifix was indeed as different as it was large.

She showed slides of the large maple timbers that her dad had helped to bolt and glue together for the piece. She spoke of her search for the wood and how God told her when she finally found it. And then how the wood had warmth and she good feel the figures and faces in the logs long before they were cut. I listened, but have to admit there were a few doubts in my mind. Besides her work was indeed different; it was a craving of the risen Christ; not the traditional crucified Christ I had always seen in churches. Within Christ's cloak were faces; traditional enough to be recognized, yet impressionist enough to provoke thought; definitely a different piece. After her presentation I introduced myself to Sister Paula.

“Sister, what next?” after working on a piece so large would anything else seem small?”

“Well, I’m not exactly sure. I think God wants me to do another large piece; possibly the back of a sanctuary. I keep seeing planks about six inches thick; but he hasn’t made it perfectly clear to me yet.”

“Do you know what kind of wood it will be?”

“Yes; I’m almost certain it will be oak.”

The family offered Sister Paula the logs; she could have as many as see wanted; and after touching and feeling each one an excited sister Paula decided she needed nearly all of them. A neighbor, abet, one a mile away from our house, had a small sawmill and rough cut the oaks into thick planks; and then helped us to transport all to her studio in the cellar of Saint Ann’s Convent on Prospect Street.

Sister Paula had too much faith to be shocked; but she may have been surprised when the calling for the wood became clear. Today in Saint Mark’s Episcopal Church on River Road in Chenango Bridge, New York is a large oak alter; its base is shaped like a boat and in the boat are Christ and the apostles. Nearby is an oak lectern shaped like the sail of a boat.

“Donnie, don’t hit those trees; they are boze’s (Gods) trees.

Coincidence? I don’t think so.

Sez It All

There once was, and maybe still is, a sign over the bar at the American Legion on Kent Street in Windsor, New York that read:

There is not much to see in a small town; but what you hear makes up the difference.

The Con

Gallagher the comedian got a lot of laughs when he described Congress as being the opposite of progress. Aside from our government I admit to having been conned more than once or twice. I further admit to being able to smile about it much more readily today than at the time of the occurrence.

The best con pulled on me occurred on the Erie Lackawanna's famous "Phoebe Snow." The Phoebe Snow was billed as the epitome of rail travel available to the working man. Each car of this train had a picture of Phoebe on the bulwark near the doors. She looked like the same girl with long blond hair, gentle but enticing eyes, and a long flowing dress that appeared on some of my grandmother's china. There were no movies on the train during the ride from Binghamton to Buffalo. You either watched the scenery out the window or stared straight ahead into the eyes of Miss Phoebe. She had to be a Miss; she looked too pure and innocent to be a Mrs. And the word Ms. Had not been invented yet. As the eldest grandson and the youthful adventurer of the family I was delighted to be selected to accompany my grandmother on a trip from Binghamton to Cleveland, Ohio, where she visited Johanna, one of her two twin sisters. Later, we would continue on to Chicago to visit Uncle George and Aunt Helen. This was the first long trip my grandma had taken in my lifetime; the first since she came over from the old country; it was an adventure for both of us.

We waited for the train in the Lackawanna station across from the Arlington hotel. The station was a delightful piece of architecture, two stories tall with a Marconi tower that still looms over the whole structure. Just looking at the building takes me back to the days of steam locomotives. The inside was paneled with wood and the seats had been polished by thousands of bottoms sliding on and off them over the years. Many of those bottoms had come directly from Ellis Island to the mines of Pennsylvania, and then, later, on to Binghamton hoping to improve their lot by gaining employment in the Endicott Johnson shoe factories. Those same families just one or two generations later, put a lot of the 'know how" into the firm we now refer to as IBM.

Grandma just sat on a bench and waited. I on the other hand was a certified seat polisher. I looked at the lunch counter with high handled soda water dispensers and then sat down. I walked over and read all of the dispatch notices and checked out the ticket agent; who still wore a visor; and then I sat down. I went outside and asked some Gandy dancers if they still used railroad torpedoes to warn Engineers of trouble down the track; and then I sat down. And every time I heard anything that remotely sounded like a train I got up and then; sat down.

I know I wasn't nervous because even today, when considered reasonably well traveled, I still get up to go watch a train; given the opportunity.

Taking a train from the foothills of the Catskills to Buffalo was much better than TV. First you got to ride over the Chenango River and view the Clinton Street Bridge; definitely more thrilling than traveling by car because this time I was going to Buffalo and not the old Philadelphia Sales discount store on Clinton Street. I remember looking into the windows of the EJ factories and out over the fields between Endicott and Owego. The further west and north we went the flatter the land got and grandma wondered if we were heading to the desert.

Once in Buffalo we had to stand and wait while the porter turned our seats around. Seems the railroad found it easier to switch all of those seats and hook an engine onto what had been the rear of our train than to turn the whole train around. Once the seats were turned the conductor stepped outside and hollered, "All aboard for Erie, Ashtabula, and points west."

It was about this time that we caught our first glimpse of the waters of the Great Lakes. Shortly thereafter a black waiter stopped by and asked if we would like anything to drink; Grandma declined, but said okay when I asked for a beer.

He asked if I was eighteen. I assured him that I was and grandma confirmed I had spoke the truth. Soon thereafter I paid $2.25 for the same size bottle and brand I had bought for quarter the night before at the Polish Club on Prospect Street. He poured that beer in a Pilsner glass making certain it had more head than beer in it. I had to wait for the foam to settle and then, just I was ready to take my first sip he came over and took both the bottle and the glass stating that, "I'm sorry sir, but we have crossed the border and you have to be twenty-one to drink in Pennsylvania." From Erie to Cleveland I had, and to this day still, I have this vision of him enjoying my beer back in the kitchen.

My Dad had always taught us that just because a man had a different colored skin doesn't mean that he is dumb. That waiter sure reinforced Dad's teaching.

Nailing It Down

Having raised four kids I am qualified to share a technique for determining if they have really washed their hair; that is once they are old enough to shower themselves. Watch the finger nails. If they have really applied suds, scratched and scrubbed it, the fingernails have to come out clean. Dirty nails, Dirty hair.

Were You There

"Were you there during the delivery?" this seems to be a prerequisite question for showing off baby pictures these days. The same guy who got nervous if you looked at his wife's ankles a few months back is now willing to show pictures of her "all" in the delivery room; becoming a parent for the first, or any time, can do strange things to a person. I was there when our first was delivered and I remember it well.

If we had been pregnant when we came home from the honeymoon we would have been happy. Would have started gossip in the town and shocked a family member or two, but we would have been happy. We had talked "family" long before the wedding.

The interviews had gone well. We had been interviewed together and separately. When the letter arrived announcing that we had been approved we were thrilled and we were also prepared to wait. Several friends who had adopted had waited as long as two years for a match. Reconciled, we were that the letter was just one more step in a long process.

Six weeks later Carole called me at work, crying; my first reaction was that someone must have run over the cat. "No, no, we are going to have a baby. "YOU ARE PREGNANT?" "Don, we are going to have a baby tomorrow. They called. They have a baby for us." Talk about a short two-year wait. "Boy or girl?" Carole couldn't remember for a moment. "Boy; I think, I can't remember. I was too excited. No, I'm sure it is a boy." Turned out she was right.

The next day we went in for a briefing. The process was designed to protect the little guy at all cost. He was to have a family that was ready to accept and love him. If Carole or I had any apprehensions the time to back out was now. For us it was an unnecessary delay. We left wishing they had brought the baby in. We were anxious, happy, a little hyper, and just ready to do it. The worst part was being unable to share the news. We were cautioned to sleep on it for one night, just in case. We were going to be parents.

The next day he was asleep in a bassinet when we first saw him. The advisor left us alone for an hour or so to get acquainted. We touched his hair, soft face, little ears and smiled at the expressions he made during his sleep. His finger tried to grab my little finger when I placed it in his hand. Both of his feet could fit in the palm of my hand. Never did I expect them to grow into the size thirteen's that would one day stretch my loafer's very time he put them on. Carole changed his diaper and he responded by proving his plumbing worked the minute the dry one was on. We held him, loved him and coo'd him from the start.

Again the process required that we wait one more day before bringing him home; but now we could tell. We really needed that day because we didn't have a thing for a baby; there had been no nine month prep time.

I drove to Olum's Furniture in Johnson City where my Dad was a salesman. "Dad, I need a crib." He told me to wait a couple of months and they would be on sale; "Get one then." "Pop, you don't understand; I need one now. You are going to be a Grandpa tomorrow." The two of us were so excited that when it was time to write up the delivery contract neither of us could remember what street I lived on. It was silly, it was dumb. It was wonderful.

Brian Peter Litchko joined our family when he was six weeks old. Today he is six-foot three and one of only two people in the family tall enough to look down at me. During the years between that bassinet and now there have been hugs, kisses and runny noses, giggles and tears, shouting matches and warm moments. Ours is a typical family and ours is a typical son.

"Litch were you there when your first was delivered?"

"You bet."

* * * * *

In Or Out

"Shut that door; you are letting the flies in; what do think this is; a barn?"

Next to the Hail Mary's my mother said when saying her rosary, "Shut the door," was her next most repeated phrase from the time school go out until the teachers recouped enough to take us back in the fall.

The kitchen was full of sweet smells and goodies as Mom canned preserves and we four kids, along with a few bee's, kept coming in because:

"I'm hot; I need a drink of water."

"Need my comic books. I'm going to trade with Patty."

"Gotta go to the bathroom!"

"You got any clothes, Mom, the dry cleaning man is coming."

And even out in the country it was "the ice cream man is coming. Mom, quick, the ice cream man."

On many days it was tough to decide if the screen door was there to keep the flies and bees in or the flies and bees out. Mom was not the only one to be tormented by this problem.

The nylon net was draped down over my helmet and the drawstrings were wrapped across my chest and around my back which brought the net tight to my shoulders. Once again fearless Don was prepared to enter the world of the honeybee. A couple puffs from my smoker at the entrance to calm them down and then a couple of more puffs across the top of hive as I removed the cover; and I was prepared to swap frames and handle several hundred of my girls, as I called them.

Bees can be fooled. They tend to always make honey in the center of a hive and work the hardest when the center is empty. A smart bee keeper rotates the frames, always keeping empties in the center. Bees can be fooled, but every now and then one can fool the beekeeper.

The first inkling I had that anything was wrong was when little legs grabbed hold of my ear. I gently flicked my veil thinking one had reached through its netting and took hold. It didn't release. Fast movements annoy bees and with a few hundred buzzing around my head it would not have been prudent to just slap myself in the side of my head to squash it. I could only stand still. Still, while she walked around the rim of my ear. Still, while her inquisitive nature took over and she took a troll inside my ear; further than any Q-Tip had ever gone. The fine fur on her body tickled me; but not to the points of giggles. Despite rumors to the contrary I had sincere doubts that she would just walk through and exit via my other ear. Concern that she might get stuck in some human earwax was genuine and the thought of a sting inside my head was even scarier. Large volumes of water can accumulate on a beekeepers upper lip at times like this.

Was I scared? Damn right, and that is probably what saved me. I was too scared to move. After an eternity she backed out of my ear and strutted over to my upper lip to take a drink. I took great care not to inhale as she explore both nostrils. Eventually she found her way to a fold in the veil where I could see her.; at which point two fingers on a gloved hand quickly squeezed and put her out of my misery.

The value of a screen is directly related to which side of the screen you are on; Mom and I know.

● ● ● ● ●

How I Stopped

The cry came from a broken heart; not a pricked finger, a grass cut or a mosquito bite. Dad's learn the difference their first day in Dad's school. The tears were so many that they made tracks down cheeks dirtied by the hands of a six year old who had played in a sand box, dragged a kitten around in a beat up doll carriage, and then planted some golden kernels so she could grow her own corn in her own garden.

"Tootser, come here. What's the matter?"

"You don't love me." (sob upon sob)

"Honey, what do you mean I don't love you? Where did you ever get that idea?"

The runny nose, tears, and dirty face being held to my chest made my white T-shirt look like marble cake batter.

"My teacher."

"Your teacher said that daddy didn't love you?"

"My teacher said that if you smoke you get cancer and die; and, if mommies and daddies really loved us they wouldn't smoke."

I never finished my last cigar. Only a six year old that loved me so much she hurt could have made me quit.

Never To Be Forgotton

Madeline Griffin was a robust lady of Italian descent who had married a cigar smoking Irishman of gentle disposition. Together they built a home adequate to house five kids and accept company any time of the day or night. Never did I go, announced or unannounced, to the Griffin home and not feel welcomed. I do recall one day when for a few moments I had doubts.

I parked my fifty-six Chevy in their circular drive and the moment I opened the door I heard boom, whomp, boom. I didn't know which one of the kids did what; but I was guessing it wasn't something very good. Boom, whomp, boom. I listened for yells; there were none. I listened for angered phrases like, "I told you darn kids for the last time," but there were none; just boom, whomp, boom.

Didn't know what they had done, but if they had been whacked so hard they couldn't even yell it was probably time for friend Don to knock on the door and give cause to interrupt the beating. I jogged to the back porch door and yelled "Hello, Donnie here; anyone home?" No response, just boom, whomp, boom; and the noise was coming from the kitchen.

I stepped onto the porch and looked into the kitchen prepared to see blood and bones. There was Madeline, knees on the floor, hands over her head clutching the biggest cast iron fry pan I have ever seen. Boom. Whomp, boom; she was beating the very dickens out of a couple of hospital white dish towels.

When Madeline made veal scaloppini it was thin, very thin, tender and delicious.

If I got whooped by that cast iron fry pan a few dozen times I'd be thin too.

At This Very Location

I recently received a historical marker for my birthday; it read "AT THIS VERY LOCATION ON APRIL 12, 1861 ABSOULTELY NOTHING HAPPENED." My problem now being where to put it; I can't think of any place in the world to put it. Something is happening everywhere, all the time. Our problem is that everyone is so darn busy they don't take the time to discover what is happening; let alone what has happened; take for instance the old Windsor Bridge.

I sometimes wonder how many people who drive over the old Windsor bridge, (Windsor, New York that is,) the one just east of the red light, ever reflect on all the excitement and history that has occurred in that short quarter mile between the bridge and the railroad underpass on down the road.

I'll bet there are people living in Windsor who never saw the bridge turn white over night in the late spring or early summer without benefit of a snow storm. I have. The bridge was lit with street lights and at certain times when the temperature, humidity, and a dozen other factors were just right the May flies would hatch and immediately migrate towards the lights. I have seen every inch the old Windsor Bridge covered with six to twelve inches of white May flies; as pretty as it was interesting. At a narrow riff below the Windsor Bridge; down near the golf course I once saw the water boil with fish when a thick hatch happened; it was all over in ten minutes; but if Uncle Joe and I didn't see a hundred fish jumping at once we didn't see a one.

So sad, what people miss, because there is so much history right there in sleepy little Windsor; for instance, on the left just as you cross the bridge, hanging out over the river was once the best tree house in Broome County; perhaps in the whole state. It was fifteen or twenty feet off the ground. There was a wood burning stove with some adequate cooking space and enough room to stretch out a couple of sleeping bags. The house was substantial enough to hold several generations of Windsor boys. When one generation of boys outgrew the need for a tree house it would go vacant for the winter months and then the next summer another group of young explorers would climb up and claim it as their own.

My cousins held access to the tree house for a summer or two and took great delight in spending Friday and Saturday nights there. The house was about level with the sidewalk on the bridge. The boys would wait in the dark for young lovers to walk hand in hand across the bridge, thinking they were alone, when suddenly a voice would yell "take your hands off of her." Many a Windsor father owes a debt of gratitude or two to my cousins. Cousin Fred took special delight in waiting for the errant drunk to cross. In the wee hours of the morning Fred would make sounds like a baby crying and watch the poor soul try to make up his mind if he had just heard Moses in the weeds along the shore of the Susquehanna.

On the right hand side of the bridge is where I docked my canoe after making a midnight run down from the big bend, up near where Occanum Creek joins the river. Several family members had been fishing up stream and when it was time to head home they walked up to the railroad tracks. I took the canoe down without aid of lantern or flashlight; another whole new experience. With only a partial moon out the shadows of the trees along the banks close in on you and the river appears to grow narrow. When you stray into the weedy shallows big carp are frightened into jumping, and fall, slapping back into the water; sometimes just inches from your paddle. Even though you know exactly what happened, and why, there is always a brief moment when your hair stands on end.

Ears are as valuable as paddles when on the river at night. The eyes, in the dark, cannot pick out the biggest "V" to guide you through the riffs and rapids. Ears tell you when you are leaving deep pools and entering fast water. Scrapping sounds and jolts on the bottom of the canoe tell you when you have guessed wrong. When, at last, you see the light on the old Windsor Bridge it is a bitter sweet vision. A part of you is glad that you made it, dry, and another part of you is sad that the adventure Is over.

Up from where I docked the canoe once stood an old carriage house where folks traveling to Binghamton from New York City via horse and buggy would stop for refreshments. The house is gone now; but the big black walnut tree might still be there. I know that tree well. Picked a bushel of walnuts there once while they were still in their green husks; woke up the next morning to find I had taken a big step toward integration. My hands were dyed black so permanent that the only way I could get them white again was to scrape layers of skin off each night with a jackknife; took me a full two weeks to become an albino again.

Mr. Bush lived a couple hundred feet from that tree and he had a good laugh over my predicament. He, too, knew the tree well as he would use the walnut tusks to dye his traps. Imagine knowing a man who made a substantial part of his living by trapping along the river as late the seventies or early eighties. These kinds of people were supposed to live in Alaska or Canada; Mr. Bush did it in Windsor; just twelve miles from downtown Binghamton. A fairly private man I knew him well enough to nod when we passed by each other on the street; but each time I saw him come up from the river I was certain that Lewis and Clark were going to walk up right behind him.

Between Mr. Bush's house and the walnut tree was Chris's gas Station. Each summer, in addition to gas, Mr Chris would lay in a supply of bamboo fishing poles, exactly like the ones you see in movies of the old south. They were always tied to the pipes that supported the canopy in front of his station. My Dad would pick out one for me each summer. I caught my first fish, a sucker, under the old Windsor Bridge. When the new Route17 Bridge was built it diverted traffic away from Mr. Chris's station and eventually he sold the place to a couple of famous agronomists; (My Godfather, Uncle Joe, and my Aunt Mary.)

Across the street from the agronomists house is now a Baptist Church. The building wasn't always a church; once it was a cannery. People from around Windsor would take the fruits of their garden and have it processed and returned in tin cans; just like from the stores; except the cans didn't have pictures or fancy labels on them. When chest freezers became affordable, most folks lost the excitement of having to open a tin can.

Prior to it becoming a cannery that same building was a Dairyman's League Creamery which I remember best because of its sounds. Each milk can had its own clang or ring; the ones with handles like hinges (knuckle busters) would ring, the ones with fixed, welded handles would clang.

Farmers would drive their trucks up a ramp and stop. The cans would be rolled with hands that expertly grabbed them by the lids; hand over hand, spinning them until the cans were on the tailgates from where they were hoisted onto a gravity fed, roller conveyor. There were scraping sounds; and sounds like buoys make out it the ocean. Each roller on the conveyor would make a whirrrrr as the milk can passed over it. Once inside the creamery you could hear the full cans bang onto one another as they came to a stop. There were more bangs when a hammer was used to knock the lids off. Then there were hisses and the sound of steam as the cans passed through the sterilizer and onto the exit conveyor.

The farmers would visit until they thought their cans were about through and then the trucks would pull up to the exit conveyor. More sounds were made as lids were matched up to the empty cans; and the matched set was tossed into the back of the pickup trucks. Rusty brakes squeaked as the trucks went down the ramp. All of this was going on at once and to be part of it was like being in the middle of a big mechanical clock. If operating today it would be a major tourist attraction. I once thought of the creamery as being part of a giant erector set; it was.

Sometime I heard swear words at the creamery when full cans of milk were returned to a farmer because an inspector found some dirt or perhaps evidence of mastitis in the can—every can was sampled.

Moving past the creamery, away from the bridge, was once a multistory feed mill. It burned down one night providing an evenings worth of excitement and several months worth of conversation.

Up near the railroad tracks was the GLF farm store. GLF stood for Grange League Federation; but I remember a lot of men joking that it meant "Gyp the Lousy Farmer." I guess maybe that's why they changed the name to Agway. I can't really comment on the prices. At age seven I didn't buy many farm supplies. I will say that the smell of all the grains, leathers, and supplies at GLF made me feel like I was a man whenever I went in the place.

All of these wonderful places, people and events, happened within a quarter mile of the old Windsor Bridge. Sure as hell can't put up one of those "Nothing Happened Here" signs on that Bridge; least ways not while I'm around.

Really A Poet

Robert Frost once lived down the road from our house; well actually about three or four miles from our house and a couple of roads over. He went to England, returned to Derry, New Hampshire, moved to Vermont and died; accomplishing all of these tasks prior to my moving into the neighborhood. I really never got to know him very well. Like many Americans I never forgot President Kennedy's smile as he looked at Robert's weather face when he rose to speak at the Presidents inauguration. Indeed the image of these two famous, and New England favorites, is forever implanted in the minds of those who watched that day.

The press claimed that Kennedy loved literature and Frost's poetry; thus Robert was invited to share in the glory of the day. I don't profess to be a scholar or critic of Frost's works; but I do have this gnawing feeling that poetry was really a cover for his real career as a political advisor. Shake your head if you want and accuse me of having a vivid imagination; but I maintain that a man who wrote articles like "Promises to Keep" and "Good Fences Make Good Neighbors," is really writing policy statements for some political party; and Kennedy knew good when he read it.

The National Park Service maintains Robert Frost's home today and I have toured it. Connoisseurs and purists "ooh and ahh" as they walk from the barn, through the wood shed and into the kitchen and living quarters. In typical New England fashion all of these functional areas were connected into a single structure. Robert never got wet when he went from the kitchen to the barn. It was reported that he was often concerned that a highwayman might have slipped into the barn while he was in the house, and so he packed a pistol when he went to milk. There was never a report that he shot the pistol; he just took comfort in having it.

I can be impressed by some of the simplest things and the most impressive thing in the Frost home (to me) was an old board. A board not polished, finished, carved, marked or inscribed; just a plain one by six about three feet long, which leans against the wall near Roberts high backed rocker. After chores Robert would come in, sit in his rocker and rock until the squeaks got into the right rhythm for his mind to work. He would then slide the board across the arms of the rocker and start to write. No lap top computer; no fancy writer's retreat house; just an old wooden rocker, a board, a tired back; and a farmer's daydreams to record on paper. That's what Pulitzer prizes and National Treasures are made from.

I never met Robert but he and his board have served me well. I have stopped putting off doing things because I don't have the latest gadget or equipment. "Doing" gets more done than "waiting until."

I have also stopped worrying about my married children's welfare to the degree I once did. Robert's grandfather worried so much about his grandson, that do nothing poet, that he gave Robert the small farm in Derry so the guy would have a legitimate way to feed his family. If Grandpa had just waited a couple of years he could have got off by just buying him a rocking chair and an old board.

WHY ROCKS? WHY NOT?

I collect a lot of things; but somewhat sporadically. Have started and stopped a coin collection a dozen times. For ten years I collected every commemorative stamp the US issued; only because the Postal Service billed me once a year and sent them automatically. I seem to collect a lot of one of kind socks; that turned out to be a good thing because when I moved to Texas and bought a pair of cowboy boots I got to use most of them. And then I pick up rocks.

Note I said pickup and not study. Some people have all consuming collections of this and that and they think that because they have them that they must become experts on all of their and that's. Not me; I pick up rocks because some are pretty, some are interesting to look at; and most of all because God put them under my feet to be noticed.

I have had sandstone from the desert near the Grand Canyon and Red Jasper from Cave Creek Arizona. Bought home enough once to fill a fish tank and that's what my brother Dick did with them. Friends give me rocks sometime. Pat Griffin gave me a trilobite that she had found on a gravel slide outside Saint Louis; it's a neat little limestone bug that happened to grow up in that part of town. Tom once gave me a stone shrimp about a foot across that he found south of Fort Worth; he called it an Ammonite. I had always thought they were a religious sect that lived near Lancaster, PA. As one who studied such things he once took me to a likely location to look for ammonites; then all afternoon, every time I got close to a rock he would yell, "Watch out for the black widows." He was right, the place was crawling with them; I remember the day well. Sometime I'd like to take him to Susquehanna PA to look for blue stone and every time he bends over I'll yell "watch out for the rattlesnake." Maybe take a few years off his life just to get even.

I have fossils of herrings that once swam in Wyoming. Found them in a rock shop in China Lake, California. On that same trip I picked up a bunch of geodes that happened to look like grenades as I entered the Ontario airport security station. I had wrapped them all up in my underwear. Each time I unwrapped one the gal who performed the search would say "Oh, look at that one." And I'd get nervous wondering if she liked the rock or happened to find a stain on my shorts.

Spent weeks trying to find some unprotected petrified wood out in the desert and later found some in an alley right behind our house; in Phoenix near a garbage can. I found a geode near the base of a butte; it was the day I learned that range steers were not as friendly as my Uncle Fred's Holsteins. I didn't have to run; but I did walk darn fast with one eye draped back over my shoulder.

I had some core samples taken from Mt Ore, Arizona. Remember tapping on the boards overhead at the mines entrance with my pistol, wanted to be certain no snakes would drop down into my pants. Friend Marty and I would stroll into the abandoned mine which was probably not wise. Would have taken years off our mothers lives had they known of our whereabouts. But on the other hand when India Jones does it everyone thinks it is just fine; he just made the movie first. My joy is that I did it.

Traveled to Herkimer, New York to look for diamonds a few times and found more than just a few. On one trip my sister-in-law Mary took the best of our finds and wedged it into her navel; created a mild stir when we stopped at Brooks Chicken House in Oneonta on our way home. I still hear them talking about her when I stop in occasionally; "Ya, she had a diamond in her navel and she lost her contacts in the John—doesn't that beat all?"

Sometimes when I'm real old I might read a book and learn about rocks. Today I can still walk and figure I better pick them up while I can.

● ● ● ● ●

Father Of The Bride

I have been the father of the bride twice. Found the experience to be both painful and fulfilling. I guess it as close mentally as a guy can get to experiencing childbirth. You really don't want to give her up, and, at the same time you are proud of what she has become; and the fact that she and her husband have what it takes to make a go of it.

Everyone treats the father of the bride with a lot of respect; telling him how good she looks, thanking him for the good time and all; and they are all worried about your health; "How you holding up old man?" Yep, everyone treated me nice except the newspaper. Newspapers never do justice to the father of the bride. Just once I'd like to scan the wedding section and read something like this:

The father of the bride wore a white on white formal dress shirt secured from Adams apple to midriff by genuine, imitation mother of pearl, cufflinks. The bottom button of the shirt was made of white plastic; and was not visible until the father tried to do a polka during the reception. Three rows of pleats on either side of the buttons provided a much needed slimming effect. Convertible French cuffs added to the formality of his attire.

His lower torso was adorned with white jockey shorts covered by traditional black tuxedo trousers. The trousers were adjustable from size twenty-two to fifty-six; an appreciated convenience as each time the father paid the cater, the bar tab, and the musicians, he was able to pull them in a notch.

The trousers were cuff-less in keeping with local tradition and finished with shiny black ribbon which expertly covered the sewn outer seam of each pant leg.

Black socks from the father's personal collection provided a nostalgic touch to the wardrobe. The socks were inserted into patent leather shoes obviously borrowed from a retired tap dancer.

A multi-pleated cummerbund eased the transition from shirt to trousers as well as camouflaging a normally visible middle age bulge. A crossed over, untied bow tie kept him sufficiently short of breath such that the family was able to control him throughout the reception.

The outfit was completed with a matching black jacket, which was as functional as decorative. The father was noticed to be slipping the stems of chocolate covered strawberries into the various pockets as he greeted guests; going from table to table. Later in the evenings fingers inserted into those same pockets would come out brown. This was attributed to the chocolate on the stems melting and was not considered to be a fault of the manufacturer.

And the bride looked nice.

George Had Gracie

Great scientific studies, undoubtedly funded by millions upon millions of hardworking taxpayer dollars, have proven what I intuitively knew all along; there are morning people and there are evening people; and I am a morning people. Further I am the onely person in our family who is a morning person. This is a mixed blessing which frequently challenges my faith. Recall the morning of 27 October 1991, from my perspective.

The clocks rolled back at 2 AM. An excellent way to start for a whale watching trip because I can get Lucas and Carole out of bed on their time and still get to the ocean by my time. I love it. I am absolutely convinced that this is the first time either of them have realized that four o'clock comes twice a day. After a half hour of "Carole, are you ready?" and "Just give me a minute, gee, you are pushy," replies, we are in the car. Carole with no shoes and Lucas with only a T-shirt; it is a typical early morning start, Fortunately, super dad had emptied a closet into the car trunk, as he knew it would be cold on the open seas. Once again he was right. Once on the road suddenly everyone is full of concern and advice:

"Boy is it ever foggy out."

"Yes, dear, that is why I wanted to leave early."

'You will have to drive slow, won't you?"

"Yes, dear, that is why I wanted to leave early."

“Maybe we should have got up earlier?”

“Yes, dear, that is why I wanted to leave early.”

“You aren’t listening to me are you?”

“Yes, dear, that is why I wanted to leave early.”

Conversations tend to be one sided in our family early in the morning. Carole goes to sleep, Lucas goes to sleep, and, I drive to Gloucester.

Carole wakes up just as I pull into town. “There it is; there is our boat.” “Carole that can’t be our boat; we need one down near the ocean.” “Well that’s the one I made the reservations for.” With a big, exaggerated sigh I swing around to go back and check. Carole is right; I could not see the channel leading to the ocean from the road. Somehow, by accident we were at the right place even though neither of us had been there before, nor had we ever heard of the place.

“Carole, dear, how did you make these reservations?” “Oh, I just called the long distance operator and told her I couldn’t find the note you left me but thought you said it was in Gloucester.” She said she watched whales once and she sounded so nice that I said ‘why not” and she made the reservations for me. Wasn’t she nice? Isn’t it a good thing I woke up what I did?”

Then for the first time I understood how George Burns felt living with Gracie all those years.

• • • • •

SPEECH 101

Speech 101, the college version of "Show and Tell," brings out creative juices in a lot of freshmen who might have been lemons all their life if not forced to stand in front of a class, or fail.

One chap started by holding up an expensive camera and asking "I'll bet you think this is a five hundred dollar camera?" When we all nodded our heads he said, "Well, you are right."

Another chap spent a half-hour teaching us how to hold a beer can by straddling the top and bottom rims with two fingers as opposed to just grabbing the can. He supported his method by explaining heat transfer principles; grasp the can and your body heat warms the beer. "Evil, evil." He then tapped the rim with his church key, to keep the foam down; this was in the days prior to flip top lids.

The best part of his pitch was his conclusion. He asked if we all understood what he had taught. We all acknowledged that we did; he really had kept us interested. "Good," he said, "Now practice," and with that he passed out a can opener and a can of brew to everyone in the class. The poor Prof was so stunned that the beer was long gone before she even thought to say no. I don't think he ever completed his freshman year at Broome Tech; but I have no doubt he is a success at something, somewhere.

Dear friend Judie tells of getting attention when she addressed the class with "I'm a hooker and my mother is a street walker."

She didn't lie. Judie hooks rugs and her Mom was a meter maid. She aced the course.

On my bucket list of things to do when I retire is, instead of watching morning talk shows, I will drive to the local college and audit Speech 101; just for the smiles.

● ● ● ● ●

History Repeats

What is the importance of canoes, trees, and Sunday afternoons? In my mind the answer is simple; that combination of variables serves to prove that history does repeat itself.

Son Lucas and I were floating down the Merrimack River; about ten miles above Concord, New Hampshire and elected to go through the only fast portion in that part of the water. Was it a snag or a bite on my line I'll never know; but I do know I should have watched the river and not my fishing pole. Suddenly we were swinging broad side in very fast and very deep water, headed right for a large oak that had fallen in the river. The two of us together were not strong enough to get control; and when we hit the tree fiberglass crunched, cross bars snapped and a twenty-five year collection of fishing gear went to the bottom as the canoe rolled over. We each came up with a life vest in one hand and the edge of the canoe in the other. History had repeated itself; only one of the characters had changed. Usually when I hit trees with canoes on Sunday afternoons it was with my brother Dick in the bow.

The Geneganslet Creek flows from up near McDonough down to the Chenango River south of Greene, New York. Smithville Flats is the only town of size on the Genny and my Uncles farm bordered the creek for better than a half mile. Dick and I had fished it, waded in it and swam in it. Most significant on this particular Sunday afternoon was the fact that we knew the previous summer the Conservation Department had built a series of small, two and three logs, dams and side dikes designed to speed up the flow in certain areas and thus improve the steam for trout.

That Sunday was the first of the New Year, the previous two days had been exceptionally warm and the January thaw had arrived early. Knowing the water would be fast and high as a result of the run off: Dick and I put on long johns, strapped the canoe on the car and headed to Smithville Flats. This was the day the Litchko boys were going to white water over the dams.

In fact we did darn good for several miles; flying over dams such that every once and a while the whole canoe would be airborne. We would hit the water with a whomp, dig in our paddles and catch the next sluice across pools where trout would be hiding in the spring. When you paddle with one person for a long while canoeing becomes an automatic experience. I never had to holler "switch" when I was tired of paddling on one side; Dick would just sense it and switch over without looking back or saying a word. When we went under low branches if Dick leaned left I automatically leaned right and balance was never a problem. Dick was more than a canoeing partner; he was my brother and we handled the white water with confidence that can only come from having been together many times before.

The Genny had few real sharp bends but we managed to find one. A ninety degree turn to the left, a short fifty feet of straight and then another ninety degree turn right. We slid around the left turn like a couple of Olympic pros and then in unison said "Oh S—t." A tree had fallen across the whole creek right on the bend. There was room to get under it; but not time to lean left and one lean right. On a gray Sunday in January, with the air temperature in the low thirties, and water about the same we rolled over in a five-foot deep pool. My toes could just touch bottom enough to keep my head above water as I bounced downstream. Exactly where we were was not certain; but we guessed it to be about a mile to the next bridge from which we could hike to Ester and John Sullivan's house. Ester, we knew, would let a couple of dripping otters stand in her kitchen while she called for our Uncles to come and pick us up.

Our seat cushion life preservers had floated away as did one paddle. The spare paddle had been strapped down so we were in good shape in that regard. By the time the canoe and we were out of the water our teeth were chattering pretty good. Field and Stream and Outdoor Life had both posted articles about what to do if one gets wet in the winter and their lessons were not wasted on us. Strip down, ring out as much water as possible, and put your clothes back on. If you keep moving your body temperature will warm you up and it is possible to survive even if it is freezing out.

So there we were; two six footers, stark naked, big wet snow flakes coming down, standing on the bank of the creek in winter; when, we hear a car.

Under these conditions would you immediately run towards the noise; flag down the vehicle and ask for help? Neither did we. We hide behind a couple of trees, waited for the car to pass; got dressed and paddled like hell for Ester's house.

Once back at the farm Aunt Jean gave us each a half glass of good brandy and we survived the experience without so much as a sniffle.

Dick and I had previously hit another tree in a little creek up near Sidney, New York. This creek developed from the base of the East Sidney dam and flowed down to the Susquehanna. Without checking a topographical map I'm guessing it dropped two or three hundred feet in elevation over the course of a couple of miles; consequently when they let water out of the dam into the narrow creek it flowed fast. We had never canoed that creek and would not have on that Sunday except that when Dad read the Sunday paper at breakfast he said "look at this, they are having Olympic qualifying white water trials up Sidney way today. Bet that would be interesting to watch." "Sure thing Dad." We could try for the Olympics just thirty miles from home. In twenty minutes we were gone with our mother yelling for us to be careful as we pulled out the driveway.

As we left the Susquehanna Valley and started the drive up towards the dam the thought did occur to us that there did not appear to be many level stretches of water until we would get back down to the Susquehanna.

At the base of the dam there were cars and spectators everywhere. Water gushed out of the base of the dam at about four million miles an hour. Riding in and out of the boulders, going through gates, (poles hanging from ropes suspended across the stream) were people with helmets on, in kayaks.

"Hey mister, where do we sign up?"

"Do you have helmets?'

"No"

"Do you have a kayak?"

"No"

"You don't"

Innocent kids that we were—we were disappointed.

"Well look, if we can't compete would you mind if we put in and took a ride?"

"It's a public steam. I can't stop you; but I should."

The first falls we went over were about four feet high and we shot straight out into clear air. Had we wings that canoe could have soared down to the Susquehanna like a glider, We stayed upright when we hit the water; but with so much force that we popped one seat right off the gunnels. Next we rode through a short gorge. Dick tried to paddle: I just held on to the edges of the canoe. To this day my knuckles are white from where the skin peeled off as we banged up against rock ledges.

True to form we rode it through the gorge and after that the rest of the trip boiled down to dodging boulders as we swept downstream. Eventually the stream broadened out and the water became swift but relatively shallow, perhaps a couple of feet at its highest. We could relax; we did; but we shouldn't have. Dick looked back to congratulate me on having made it through and when he did we hit a submerged log. The canoe swung around and then wedged against the log with water pouring into it. (Fortunately the old Grumman aluminum canoe could take a licking and keep on floating.) We could go nowhere without getting out; in disgust and silence we just sat there. Then brother Dick said "Piss on this;" stood up and proceeded to do just that.

When the cheers started coming we realized that several people having watched our exciting fly away at the dam, had driven down stream to a little bridge to watch our bodies float by. Now they were watching Dick.

Neither Dick nor I ever attended a big name engineering college; but we know a lot about fluid dynamics. It is easier for a log to stop canoe in mid stream than it is to stop Brother Dick in mid stream.

On a serious note, for the sake of those who might be tempted to try white water adventures, DO IT; but leave seat type and pillow type life preservers at home. If you can't afford a fishing vest type or one that guarantees to keep your head above water should you get knocked out don't go. And don't get one so bulky that you can't move—Free hands are worth a lot in fast water.

And to parents who read this and say "I would never let my kids do anything that stupid;" a thought. You can keep them close to home thinking they are safe under your wings where they can sneak and experiment with things like drugs when bored; or you can let them stretch themselves to the limit; making life so exciting that they don't have the time to get into that kind of trouble; and learn to survive in the process. My Bothers and I, to a man; thank our parents for being concerned and scared enough to worry; and trusting enough to let us try.

Tarantulas I Have Known

The number of tarantulas roaming around Trim Street in Kirkwood, New York is severely limited. I lived there for better than twenty years and only saw one in the flesh. My Uncle Joe had plucked that one from a bunch of bananas that had been delivered to his store.

Yet, despite the lack of youthful exposure, three or four tarantulas have made my life a little more interesting and I take pride in our relationships.

The second tarantula I met was at Arizona State University. The professor's name was something like Dr. Sukie (sp?); I do recall his life work centered on venomous critters and insects. His subjects include cobras, rattlesnakes, black widows, and the like, all very close up; which may account why he only had five students that semester. It was one of his larger classes: rumored to have started with twenty. I think if you survived the four years graduation was automatic.

The good doctor was kind enough to conduct lectures for Easterners who wanted to walk the desert in relative safety and learn the ways of sand, quiet, and remotely wild. He was talking my language. The lecture hall had tiered seating and was full. The doctor immediately got the crowd's attention by blowing up a large balloon and then trying to bite it to make it pop. Nobody could do it. He then turned loose a four-foot rattlesnake on a lab table and provoked it into striking the balloon; fast and IMPRESSIVE; "POP." He never even told the snake to "open wide." Being a doctor I thought he should have just to maintain tradition.

Next, he let a big, long legged, hairy tarantula crawl out of his shirt pocket, around his neck, up and down his arms while he explained that tarantulas had an undeserving bad reputation. Their venom is only as toxic as a bee sting. Their jaws, however, are so powerful that they indeed can pinch and hurt. Their temperament, however, is so gentle that they truly make good pets. The crowd was spell bound as he walked down to the first row and encouraged folks to pet his hairy friend. This guy should have been a preacher, so convincing was he; even the most timid were persuaded to touch. All was going well until one young man brushed the tarantula a might to hard and it fell onto the lap of someone who instinctively yelled and stood up. This naturally dumped the poor tarantula down among all the seats. The first three rows emptied out faster than if someone had yelled "RAID" at a local pool hall.

People went up seats, on seats, over seats; people climbed on people, over people and through people. The poor doctor was darn near trampled when he dove headlong on the floor trying to save his hairy friend. The chariot race in the movie Ben Hur was exciting, but it ranks second in my mind when compared to what I witnessed in that lecture hall.

Maybe it was good the doctor was not a preacher.

The good doctor's lessons were not wasted and I took many walks in Arizona deserts without encountering any harm.

Years later; when I transferred to Texas the family took delight in the wild tarantula who had taken up residence beside our front door. We enjoyed him, or her, (we didn't enjoy enough to ever check which) and he seemed to enjoy us; even tolerating Carole when she would chase him up the sidewalk with a broom so that nervous guests could enter the house. He was almost as effective as a watchdog, cheaper to feed, and I never had to invest in a tarantula pooper-scooper.

Tarantulas can be equalizers. My son Brian proved that when he was six years old. The drive from Windsor to the facility I worked at in Johnson City was about a twenty mile trip; far enough that you just didn't run into town three of four times a day. It was Saturday, I had to go in to check on a life cycle test, and Brian needed new shoes. I took him with me.

Fear takes many forms. Some of those forms appear in the manner of vice presidents who intimidate; men big in stature, big in authority and power, and men who could end a career just by looking at you. The firm I worked for was blessed with just one such VP and he was to visit our General Manager that same Saturday morning; and I'll admit when he came to visit on a Saturday it made people nervous.

So here comes Litch, with a six year old in tow; right into the main lobby; being a secured facility I couldn't take him into the plant, and I sure couldn't leave a six year old alone out in the parking lot. What kind of a parent would do that?

I sat Brian down in a corner of the lobby; gave him a copy of Aviation week and told him to look at the airplane pictures; "Daddy will be right back."

The guard took one look and said "Don, you can't leave the kid alone out here; we are having high level visitors this morning."

I tell the guard, "I'll only be five minutes. Watch him and I'll have him out of here before they arrive." Most reluctantly he tells me to "make it a damn fast five minutes." I could sense his fear and I move out fast. Unfortunately, not fast enough.

By the time I get to the lab the phone was ringing; "Litchko get your kid out of here NOW."

The VP had entered the lobby just after I had entered the factory. He set down his brief case while he signed the register and exchanged pleasantries with the guard; while waiting for our GM to come out and greet him. Unnoticed a six year old sitting in the corner became intrigued with the fancy leather brief case; his Dad only had a plastic one. He walked over to inspect it and while there left his Philadelphia Sales special rubber tarantula sitting on the handle. Being the well mannered little boy that I had raised; he quietly returned to his seat.

To quote the guard, "He s—t his pants," and I didn't think he was talking about Brian.

Fear takes many forms. David slued a giant with a slingshot. Brian slued a giant with a ten cent rubber tarantula.

Never Say Never

The importance of positive reinforcement and the need to persist are among the things stressed in modern parental guide books. My parents and family may not have had such formal training in these attributes but managed to get the message across by example. It seldom occurs to me that "it couldn't be done." In our house it was only a matter of how bad you wanted it that decided "it couldn't be done."

My Dad never completed high school. His dad died when he was ten; by the time he would have been a freshman or sophomore he was "farmed out" to do chores and work at a rest home for employees of Endicott Johnson Corp; run by Miss Grace Wagner in Kattelville, NY. From that time until he was twenty-six his income supported his mother and siblings. Many of the beautiful tall trees that now surround the home on Kattelville Road were planted by my Dad.

He was not an architect, or engineer, and he never worked in the construction trades; and obviously had no father or older brothers to teach him; but so long as he was my Dad, and for years prior, he just did what needed to be done. When it was time to replace the dirt floor in the cellar of the old Murphy farmhouse, which he and Mom had purchased, and replace the stone walls with cinder blocks; he just thought about it and did it. I remember him jacking up the whole house; cutting some locus posts down in the woods and them using them to hold up the place while he worked. I remember there being so much water under the house that those posts actual sprouted leaves and little branches. I remember him killing a big spotted adder(probably a milk snake) that had taken residence in the old stone foundation; he found it as he hauled those walls out; stone by stone. He was clever when he broke up tons of the those stones with a sledge hammer, until there was a six inch layer over the cellar floor making an improvised French drain before he covered them with concrete that he mixed by hand. And how it was so smooth and dry that for years thereafter we kids would roller skate around the old coal furnace on rainy days; where once there had been a cellar swamp. I remember him getting frustrated almost to the point of tears when trying to lay his first cinder block absolutely level and square, because the mortar was drying out before he got it right; and he didn't want to waste it. I also remember how proud he was when he lowered the house back down on the new foundation and no plaster had cracked; and all was perfectly level.

The one thing I can't remember is him ever quitting. If it needed to be done and the only obstacle was money, time and again Dad would show us what a little ingenuity and a lot of labor could accomplish.

My Dad taught by example; and even at eighty-one, with failing health, poor eye sight and hearing he still taught us how to exit the world with love and good grace. The day before he died he was singing "This is the day. This is the day, that the Lord has made, that the Lord has made; Let us rejoice, Let us rejoice and be glad in it, and be glad in it;" for the nurses at Lourdes hospital.

"If you want to write a book; think about it and then do it." I'm writing Dad; I'm doing it.

Folk Tales

Folk tales are interesting because there are a lot of interesting folks. Some folks accept folk tales as being gospel; which is okay as long as they don't force their religion on me.

The very words "folk tales" conjure in our minds visions of West Virginia moonshiner's, Vermont mountain men with beards hanging down to their knees, or maybe, a Maine sea captain, with a pipe in his mouth, at work mending a fish net. Never do the words "folk tales" provoke images of an aisle seat in airplanes, and yet, I maintain the cruelest occasions of my life occur when being assigned an aisle seat, and, are a result of a modern day folk tale.

Every time I get a new secretary, and over forty years I have had a few, she inevitably walks into my office, proud as a peacock and announces that she made my reservations and "I got you an aisle set because you have long legs."

Why, pray tell, does anyone want an aisle seat; save for old men with prostate problems.

If you sit in an aisle seat you have to buckle your seat belt at least three times because even though the plane might be half empty at least two smart people will want the inner seats next to you. If I were one of only three people on a 747 I bet that I would have to buckle my seat belt three times.

If you sit in an aisle seat you get bumped with brief cases, carryon bags, junk that people think is much too valuable to travel below; these same people will throw it away two weeks after they get home. You get whacked with book bags, pocket books big enough to support camping expeditions, and bottoms. Yes, I said bottoms. I defy anyone to sit in an aisle seat and not have at least one fat bottom get stuck in your face when two people try to pass, or one bends over to stuff something under the seat across the way. The space under the seat in front of you is small so naturally you tend to stick one foot out in the aisle where it will get stepped on, kicked, and ran over by the beverage cart. We don't have to worry about food carts anymore.

Sit in an aisle seat and you get to wiff bored two year olds that walk up and down the aisle with their pants full. As a four time emptier of two year olds pants I know of what I speak. This is reason enough not to take an aisle seat.

Yet the myth is so strong that long legged men desire aisle seats that I even know a few long legged men that actually think they want them, but have no idea why.

It is all because of folk tales, that's why. A tale that was repeated so long and so often that folks accept it as being the truth long after its usefulness has expired.

The tale started in my life time; prior to the days of sexual equality; back in the days when airlines knew how to make money. In those days there was no such thing as flight attendants; there were only stewardesses. And, stewardesses were always young, shapely and dressed to accent their God given figures. Never did you get served by some gal who would never see a twenty-eighth birthday again; or some Air Marshall pretending to care if we want sugar in our coffee. Service was provided by some very attractive young ladies; period; so attractive that many men would withstand the inconvenience of an aisle seat in order to audit the customer service.

So how did this folk tale get started? Like this: A guy goes to the ticket counter, beat, tired from his time on the road; dreading facing his boss in the morning because his results were far from adequate. The only thing this guy had to look forward too is a chance to audit the customer service, so he asks for an aisle seat. The agent knows aisle seats stink and immediately asks, "Why do you want an aisle seat?"

The poor tired bloke says exactly what is on his mind without thinking; "Legs."

The agent is startled by his admission and repeats it loud enough for the whole airport to hear; "You want an aisle seat to look at legs?" The guy has to come up with something quick in order to save face so he says; "No, I want an aisle seat because I have long legs."

Because of one liar and of others who heard, admired his quick thinking, and then started to use the same excuse; a folk tale was started and I have been made to suffer numerous aisle scat assignments.

I do have long legs. Aisle seats stink, and I have yet to see a male flight attendant that makes accepting the assignment worth it.

Snakes

In order to be considered a genuine, honest to goodness, outdoor person you must be committed to telling a snake story or two. Not a hiker, camper, hunter, nor fisherman can you be unless you can “rattle” on about snakes for at least a minute or two. True outdoorsman expertise is directly related to how long and how venomous the snake in your stories.

You can have been born in a New York City tenement and stayed there all your life; may never have seen the sun; have no idea who LL Bean is, and have skin as pale as 2% milk; but if you can tell a good snake story you are a outdoorsman; simple as that.

Half way between the house and the barn, along one side of the rutted driveway was a small single door structure that was nearly surrounded by wild bamboo and perhaps one lilac bush. Built of wood and sitting on a layered rock foundation the little building straddled a deep foul smelling pit. It was the pit that gave the building its purpose. I thought my grandparents to be rather well off; theirs was a three “seater” and the holes were cut in a single piece of pine, with no knots. To add to the grandeur it had a wooden floor; planks going from the door to underneath the bottom of the seat bench. There were cracks between the planks and you could see some dirt in them. The facility was complete with a pail of lime in one corner and not only a Sears Roebuck catalog; but a couple of Life magazines as well. Maybe it wasn’t the proverbial brick s—t house, but it was substantial.

Four or five years old, I'm the lone occupant and in possession of the center hole. Shirt tail pulled up in back and pants down around my ankles. I was in due process when right under the door, down one of the cracks comes a snake. Oh it might have been a garter snake, a grass snake, or brown snake, but when you are four years old, scared and it was between you and the only exit; it was a deadly spotted adder.

At least a foot of it had snaked its way down the crack with no tail yet in sight. "Somebody help me." I shouted so loud my lungs hurt.

"You are a big boy now; you can wipe yourself." The kitchen door slammed; there would be no help.

Now the snake was at least two feet down the crack and headed for my pants; and still there was no tail in sight. It is not easy to jump up and straddle the holes of a three seater when your feet are hobbled with a pair of blue jeans down around your ankles; but it can be done.

I learned self control that day. After that I could stay with my grandparents for a month at a time and never go to bathroom. I truly never did see the head and tail of that snake at the same time. I hope it fell in the pit.

Truth is that I have never seen a live rattlesnake in the woods of the Catskills or the fields of Texas though I have spent ample time in both. Got real excited once in Arizona when I found sidewinder tracks in the desert sands; but never found the snake. Did come close once when fishing the Cannonsville Reservoir north of Deposit, New York.

Barefoot, I was casting spinners and working the shoreline one evening. No need to watch where I was walking; my feet just found their own way while I kept my eyes on the water;

watching for that one trout that was going to take my lure and clear the surface before it even pulled line.

My toes kind of felt their way in the sand, mud and sometimes little pools of water. Once in a while they would find a rock or stick and then step on and balance while my other foot swung over.

The message went from my foot to my brain in an instant. It wasn't a rock and it wasn't a branch. It was round and spongy and it rolled under my foot as my weight came down on it; and it didn't crunch like drift wood.

To clear six foot from a standing position does not require a great athletic ability; only proper motivation. The snake was dead and some so and so is probably still laughing and wondering how many people got scared when they came upon the coiled snake. I know of only one.

Seeking Converts

A fine group of dedicated men once formed an organization known as the Men's Club of Our Lady of Lourdes Church in Windsor, New York. This fine, dedicated group decided to sponsor a parish raffle; the goal being to reduce the parish debt. Our Lady of Lourdes had just moved into a new, beautiful structure on Kent Street and along with a new mortgage was a need for many new implements.

In order to make the raffle a success a small group of decision makers agreed that the prize had to be something that would appeal to everyone. A thousand dollar first prize was deemed adequate.

"If prizes were sold for five for a dollar folks would think they were getting more for their money." The decision makers all agreed.

Then one member offered, "What if we offer incentives to parish members to sell chances?" "What do you have in mind?" we asked. It was a novel thought. Seems that he who made the suggestion was experienced in procuring large quantities of liquid refreshment; so he went on; "We could give them a quart of Black Velvet for every twenty-five books of chances they sold; it won't drain much from the profits."

That small group of dedicated men then proceeded to conduct one of the best, if not the most successful raffles ever held in that church. Parishioners were taking fifty books at a clip.

Several sold two hundred books. Success breeds success and this raffle was definitely a success.

The Sunday after the drawing Father announced the winners and the profits; the congregation clapped and cheered. He then most discreetly mentioned that those who were entitled to sales awards would be able to pick them up next Sunday after the nine o'clock Mass; "Vic's van will be at the rear of the parking lot out back."

Come next week Vic's van was indeed behind the church with about five cases of Black Velvet in it. Father again mentioned it discreetly along with the other parish announcements.

During the Mass the clouds turned gray and God dispensed some of his own liquids on the town of Windsor. Vic, wanting to get the raffle stuff over and done with, correctly assessed that the winners would not want to walk in the rain to pick up their awards; so he quietly drove around and carried all five cases just inside the main entrance of the church.

"The Mass is ended; go in peace:" and go they did. One man went out the door with eight bottles; many went with three or four; nearly every family went home with one. We were all walking to our cars about the time all of the other congregations in town had completed their services and were driving by "Our Lady of Lourdes."

The parish grew in numbers and many gave credit to Father Hobbs and Father Zedor for their loving attention and care.

I think, however, that some of the credit should go to the Men's Club. It didn't take long for word of our holy water to get around in a small town like Windsor.

Cow Horns

After twenty—five years I had the good fortune to renew an old friendship with Jim Thompson, a trumpeter of respectful note who was currently playing with the Atlantic Symphony. Over a couple of bottles of dark ale Jim shared what it is like to play with some of the most renowned orchestras in the world; and the reception received on various continents. Jim had also played the trumpet solos during the Olympics in Atlanta.

Jim's most favorite reception occurred in a small town in upstate Vermont. He and his family had rented a cottage for a couple of week's vacation to enjoy the peace and beauty of the country. Somehow Jim made contact with the town bandmaster; who I think ran the local hardware store. Jim asked if he could sit in for the Friday night concert when all the locals played in a gazebo on the village green. The gent was concerned if Jim could adequately read music, because he had been band master for many summers and obviously had an obligation to the town to do right by his music.

Come Friday night the band assembled on the green with the gazebo as picturesque as a calendar photo; but there was something wrong with the picture. Despite all the cars parked around the green; there were not many people on the green. The band started to play and it didn't take long for the band master to give Jim encouraging nods of approval. Having just returned from a European tour Jim was pleased to know he had made the cut. Once the piece was finished instead of clapping the applause came in the form of honked car horns; the whole town tooted and tooted.

After having played in Mexico, Asia, Canada and Europe in formal settings for audiences that were most often schooled in the classics Jim found the spontaneity of the car horns delightful.

It gave him that "Only in America, gee it is great to be back home feeling." The folks in a little Vermont town obviously had made a lasting impression on him.

A couple of days later I was telling a coworker and fellow New Englander about our reunion. I tried to relate what those car horns meant to Jim. Norm paused, after hearing my story and then said; "Litch, I wouldn't want you to burst your friends bubble, but you know in Vermont they do the same thing when there is a cow in the road."

He was right of course; but in retrospect I think Vermont might be one of the few places on earth where the music of Bach, played by expert musicians could be listened to with the same appreciation as viewing a cow strolling down a dirt road on a crisp autumn day.

I find the thought of both to be rather comforting.

What A Way To Go

There were enough children in the family to start an army. I only knew one of them well, as we worked together. We both lived in the Binghamton area; the rest of her family lived down near Scranton.

Their mother died at the age of ninety-two as I recall. Due to the need for some business travel the only way for me to pay my respects was to be at the funeral parlor the moment it opened for the first viewing. I drove to Scranton and was the first guest to join the family.

The funeral director took my coat; I signed the register and enter the parlor; walking directly to the casket. Glancing sideways I thought I detected a smile on one of the male family members face; probably because he noticed someone he had not seen in a while.

I knelt down, blessed myself, and started to say a silent prayer; "Our father who art in heaven," and was interrupted by what I thought was a smirk.

"Thy kingdom come, thy will be," and now I heard a chuckle that could not be ignored. In such a time of hurt and sorrow I was certain it was I who was the source of the humor. I'm kneeling there wondering if my socks didn't match; if the crotch was ripped in my pants. Even wondered if some fool had put a note on my back before I left work; one can get such thoughts gets in such a situation.

“As it is in heaven;” Behind me it was laugh, smirk, chuckle, chuckle.

“Give us this day our daily;” and I heard more of the same only louder. I couldn’t concentrate on my prayer; she would have to get to heaven on her own. I blessed myself, got up, and walked right past my friend, without speaking, and found the rest room.

My socks did match. My pants weren’t torn and there were no notes on my back. Damn it; I was all okay; what the hell were they laughing at?

Back to the parlor I edge up to my friend; offered a few kind words and then asked “Your Mom is not even cold yet; what’s so funny?”

“How do you think she looks?’

“For ninety-two she looks like an angel.”

‘How do like her dress?” She was dressed in a very tasteful pink gown covered with a fine net; almost like lace.

“She looks fine; whoever picked out the gown made a fine choice.”

“What about her veil?” I hadn’t paid much attention to the veil while at the casket; was more concerned about why they were all laughing at me. On second glance she did indeed have a veil over her face coming from a head piece whose material matched the gown.

“Very nice; you don’t often see that anymore.”

Now with tears in her eyes she tells me that finding a veil to match the gown only an hour before the public viewing was no easy trick.

It seems that when all of her siblings got together one of them remember that their Mom wanted to be buried wearing a veil like they did over in the old country. For a few minutes they were stumped; where in all of Scranton could you find a matching veil in so short a time; if at all.

With tears of laughter she blurted out; "My Mom may have a veil on her head; but she is bare assed in that casket."

Soup-Er

Put a teenager who speaks with slurs and has trouble with the English language, (in this case a waiter at a local restaurant,) and a women who insists on hearing only what she wants to hear, (in this case my wife,) together and the simple task of ordering a meal takes on comic proportions that exceed anything Hollywood could ever offer. The fact that it really happened only adds zest to the experience.

I had won a gift certificate to a local Italian eatery. Came home and surprised my wife and son with a "Hey, what's say we go out to eat tonight?" received no argument from either of them, and off we go in the best of spirits.

I ordered an individual pizza and Lucas ordered his thing; both while waiting for Carole to make up her mind; a practice for which both Lucas and I are accustomed.

To fully appreciate the conversation about to be conveyed the reader is advised to read the "said he," parts very fast while doing you best imitation of an New England Italian twang. Don't worry if you can't do it very well; neither could the waiter.)

Said she, "I would like the lasagna please.'

Said he, "It comes with a soupersalad."

Said she, "I don't think I can eat that much."

Said he, "So you just want the lasagna?"

Said she, "No I would like a salad with it."

Said he, "okay, like I said it comes with a soupersalad."

Said she, "I can't eat a super salad."

Said he, "But the soupersalad comes with the meal."

Said she, now getting irritated, "I don't care I just want a regular salad."

At this point son Lucas is beginning to get hungry and decides to act as an interpreter. I quickly give him a "stay out of it" stare and we both become rapt listeners. My thinking that someday this kid will get married and should know what thirty years of mealtime conversation can be like.

Said he, "So now you don't want the lasagna, just the salad?" Now his irritation is beginning to show.

Said she, "You mean I can't order lasagna with a salad; it has to be a super salad or nothing? I never heard of such a thing."

Reader, please bear in mind that this was a serious conversation between two intelligent people; not a battle of wits.

I ate my pizza. Lucas ate his and an hour later Carole got her lasagna and salad. And the waiter experienced a marriage type encounter without ever taking vows or going away for marriage preparation classes. I do think I did him a favor.

Tractor Power

Give a child a two wheeler and it becomes an instrument of independence. In my case independence started with a scooter. There was little traffic on Trim Street when I was a kid and the best place to scoot was on the road in front of our house. The lawn was lined with sugar maples, one of which was our favorite climbing tree; all of which provided shade over the roadway. To push off with one foot, pick up a little speed and try to make figure eight's on the hot road tar without losing your balance was considered quite a trick.

My first bike was great. It did everything the scooter did, but with greater speed and the flexibility of distance. No more was I restricted to "no further than the last tree on the lawn." I could explore: and tended to explore the most in front of homes whose kids did not yet have bikes.

It didn't take too long for the rest of the neighborhood to become mobile. The novelty of the bike wore off and by age eleven I was humbled into just being one of the kids again. My ego suffered a bit until my Uncle's decided that with proper training they could both boost my morale and utilize the services of their oldest nephew. "Come on up to the farm and we will teach you how to drive the tractor."

Drive the tractor. Drive the tractor. The tractor was the strongest piece of machinery on the whole farm. It could plow, pull hay wagons, carry the mower, and power the blower, which blew chopped corn to the top of the silo. It could drive over rocks, through cow flops and go right through that mess that is behind every dairy barn in the world. It could do all those things and I was going to be the one to drive it. Not every eleven year old could do it, you know. If it hadn't been for the fact that I was among the tallest eleven year olds in the country my feet might not have been long enough to reach the brake and clutch; an important factor I can assure you. This was not a riding mower or one of those let's pretend I'm a weekend farmer tractors. No sir; this was a Ferguson.

What a powerful, versatile piece of machinery. The seat could be flipped up so that rain or dew from the previous night would drain off and allow you to sit dry in the morning. The hood was gray and long. There were latches on each side which when unsnapped allowed it to be swung up and hung off the front of the tractor; thus giving access to the gas tank, the battery and radiator; which was best viewed by draping myself over the steering wheel while tiptoe balancing on top of the gear box. Each of the front wheels were mounted to a sliding axel bar such that the distance between them could be adjusted to fit exactly between rows of corn for cultivating. The monster rear wheels were mounted on reversible hubs such that the spacing between them could also be adjusted. There was an individual brake for each rear wheel that could be used to help make tight turns and may a time allowed me to jockey out of the mud holes I was always tempted to cross. The shifting lever sat between my legs much like the stick on old fighter aircraft. I would sometimes drive that tractor with the mindset of the Red Baron. The gas lever was mounted on the steering column; it slid across a notched plate that held it fast at any desired speed. In the back was a three point hitch with a hydraulic lift; and a draw bar that could hoist plows out of the ground without you ever having to stop and get off the seat. Tucked in the back near the rear axle was the power take off; a splined shaft that when attached to equipment could make mower blades shuttle back and forth, bailer's crunch up and tie hay, and manure spreaders spread.

Just imagine what it was like to be eleven years old, putting your foot on the running board in front of the clutch lever; grabbing the steering wheel and hoisting yourself up into the driver's seat; and know that you were in charge of it all. The other kid's could have their bikes. I had my ego back; pronto.

Strong; was that machine strong! Strong enough to knock the milk house off of its foundation; I sure proved that right quick when I got reverse and the first gear confused. My Uncle Fred must have thought it was strong too; because he came out of the milk house in one big hurry; I remember.

I also remember watching the disks slice the dirt just ahead of the plows and being able to drive in a straight line across fields by just watching the plow dig in and turn over dirt; never had to look ahead or in front of the tractor. I remember the fresh sweet smell of soil and the bumpy rides when the tractor pulled drags across the plowed ground. I can still hear the mower blades; those V-shaped plates that had been filed sharp by my grandfather and riveted to a shuttle bar. Best was the rhythm it made when you started cutting a ten acre plot.

I loved to mow; starting on the outside edge of a field and going round and round, working my way into the center. When it came time for the last pass I liked it best when one of my Uncles would drive. I would then sit on top of the hood up near the front of the tractor wearing a wide brimmed straw hat that had a green piece of plastic sewn on in the front of the brim; sort of like a sun visor. One of my Uncles would drive and mow slow; with reason.

All of the animals and birds that had made homes in the hay fields would keep moving and hiding in the last swath of standing hay. Now, when we mowed that last swath they had no choice but to flush. Swallows with jet like wings would dive at the tractor and me; coming within inches, trying to scare us away. Pheasants would run to the edge and try to outrun the tractor; suddenly taking to the air with their ring necks and beautiful tail feathers showing all their colors. Woodchucks would quickly waddle out of the hay and dive into the nearest hole. Those same holes would sometimes gobble up the front tires forcing the steering wheel to spin so quickly that many a time I came home with a mildly sprained thumb or wrist. I would never say a thing for fear someone would think I was too young to drive. The creatures I enjoyed the most when making that last cut were the bunnies. They would run out and zigzag in every direction. I would have my own field day jumping off the tractor; chasing and trying to catch them; every year with some success.

I would run, jump, dive, and try to get them; using my hat as a trap. The straw hat could be folded and I'd lift them up and hold them against my chest. The little animal's heart would be beating and its chest heaving after the run. I remember talking to them, petting them, and watching them calm down. Slowly I would open the hat thinking that the bunny might be able to be tamed; but only for the instant that it took that rabbit to realize it wasn't hurt and could still jump. Poof, out of the hat it would hop and then run straight line for the edge of the field.

I never drove a stock car or a racer; but I know just how a driver feels when he wins. I remember having a hundred bales on the field and seeing dark clouds roll in with lightning and thunder attached. How we would set the accelerometer at a slow speed, aim the tractor across the field, jump off and let the tractor drive its self while the three of us would run and toss on bales. I remember anxiety while sitting high on the load of hay, racing the wind down the road to the barn. The joy of pulling into the mow and getting under cover just as the first big drops left marks on the stones lining the ramps up to the barn door. And the little celebrations we had reaching down into the spring vat in the milk house and pulling out a bottle of root beer that had been stashed away for just such an occasion.

I remember it all. The feelings, the smells, the power, sights and the precious luxury of having time to think and dream during the hours I drove that tractor.

Men, they say, are crazy to work such long, hard hours trying to make a go of it on small dairy farms; and today most of them are long gone.

I know and remember; still there are times when I regret never having been that crazy.

Most Regular Guy

A Boston radio station was conducting a contest aimed at finding "the most regular guy." I self nominated by saying I ate bran flakes every morning; at my age it helps.

The Freshman Float

Question: If you allow your daughter to have the freshman class float built in your garage do you still have to tell her that you love her. I did. I do; but I don't think I should have to.

Euphoria abounds when she and couple friends announce that this year's theme for Homecoming is "IT'S A SMALL WORLD AFTER ALL;" and that they have a whole month to build it. It won't be in the garage for too long; and this year the freshmen are going to win the prize; but we have to keep it a secret."

This is a relatively easy secret to keep because for the first weeks nobody on the freshman float committee can agree on what to put on the float. I must give credit though; they did an admirable job of conning the next door neighbor out of his snowmobile trailer for use as the basic means of conveyance.

By the beginning of the fourth and final week; be it by dominance of a single strong personality, or near panic, the decision was made to have flowers and a path leading up to a real windmill; like in Holland in the spring. Can't you just see it; almost like the Philadelphia Flower show; with a pretty girl in a gown carrying a parasol. Walking on the path; "Can't you just see it?" Of course each member of the committee envisions herself in the gown, standing on the float as being her contribution to the picture. "And maybe we could even make the windmill turn." It is about this time that Dad is brought into the picture for the second time. Up to now it has been simple; he just parks his car outside for three weeks and walks in the rain, while his neighbor's trailer dominates both bays of a two car garage because "we have to have room to walk around it when we are working."

Now dad becomes a designer, carpenter and advisor with only five days to go.

Day Five and counting:

I walking into the garage to find my neighbors once black trailer being painted an ugly pea green with a brown two foot wide strip wiggling sort of diagonally across it. "Did you ask Gary if you could paint it?" "Dad, we only have four days left; we don't have a choice." Six heads all nod in agreement. Obviously the float committee made a conscious decision that the end justifies the means.

Day Four and counting:

I come home to find no freshman committee; but a humongous pile of scrap wood, of which no two pieces look alike, piled in the middle of my driveway. "Sarah's Dad said we could use it and we didn't have to bring it back. Obviously Sarah's dad didn't want to pay a dumping fee at some recycling center. We thought it would save us money because we used the money the class gave us for the float to buy refreshments for the committee. (In eight years this committee will be drinking three cocktails for lunch at the taxpayers' expense.) Seems Sarah's dad also got rid of the two cans of ten year old paint that he had felt too guilty to throw out. And my place is beginning to look like an annex to the local landfill.

Day Three and counting:

I come home to face three sullen faced committee members. My tools are scattered all over the place and a single question is phrased; "How can wc do this?" The father figure skips his supper, cuts, measures, hammers, while saying dirty words under his breath; and by midnight the skeleton of a windmill that really turns; providing they can find some little kid brother to hide inside and manually turn the axle.

Day Two and counting:

No committee, just one disgruntled daughter. "Where is your help?" "Sarah's mother took her shopping; Jeanne couldn't get a ride. Martha's mother told her she had stay home tonight if she wanted to go to the dance tomorrow night. And if they don't bring the plants this will look like a pile of you know what; and if we do win the trophy I'm going to keep it because I've done all the work." (And to think that just this very morning when I walked into the office my manager had asked me "Where were you last night? You look like hell.)

Day One and counting:

After two midnight nights we are still painting sticks and stapling on plastic flowers. It almost stands a chance; just one more midnight night.

THE DAY:

The sun shines. The entire committee shows up and they are all so proud of what "they" had done. A little brother is crammed inside the windmill and the blades start to turn. The washed station wagon pulls the float via back streets to the staging area; not an easy trick in Windsor, New York; there aren't that many back streets. All is well with the freshman class.

They might have won had not the little brother lost his footing when the station wagon stopped up near Bennett's grocery store. He fell over, along with the windmill. Windsor folks were good about rushing to pick up the pieces of the windmill and the pieces of the little brother so that the parade could resume.

An Afterthought:

The freshman float committee is a lot like giant aerospace corporations. One engineer puts a good simple design on the back of a napkin and a dozen lesser engineers jump on the bandwagon to improve it, and share in the credits, while creating a thousand drawings and thousands more technical specifications.

Marketing people, dreaming of large commissions, tell the world how good this invention is.

The whole factory celebrates when the contract is finally awarded.

And then, the next day someone asks, "How the hell are we going to build this thing?"

And some program manager turns on his computer and types the words; Six Months and counting.

● ● ● ● ●

We Should Thank Them

Had chance to think through an interesting process recently; thanks to two young friends having invited Carole and I to their wedding. The wedding came together without a flaw. The bride was on time; the groom didn't faint. The little flower girl didn't run to her mother and start crying in the middle of it all. To this point is has been a picture perfect wedding.

I predict, however, that all heck is about to break loose; just as it has for every couple that ever got hitched. Now is the time when they have to write those blessed "Thank you" notes.

"Thank You" for the finger towels, tooth pick holders, and at least one wedding gift from some other couples closet; that they didn't like and were delighted to have a way of getting rid of it.

With, almost certainty they are already late in sending out a "Thank You" to at least one relative. (Everybody has at least one old spinster Aunt who thinks that out of great respect for her they should have delayed the honeymoon until they sent her; "her card." The kids might be taking only a two day honeymoon, but in her eyes they are "late."

And then to add fuel to the fire; when they open their gifts they will cross up and place the right card on the wrong gift. Somehow one or two will get mixed up and they will end up thanking someone for the wrong thing; and Lord knows that they must thank everyone for the right thing because if they don't they will be labeled as cold and unappreciative young snots for the rest of their lives.

I don't know who started this "must send thank you notes" for wedding gifts thing; but I am convinced it is wrong; one hundred and eight degrees out of phase wrong.

Think about it. A newlywed couple has much more interesting things to do evenings than to write thank you cards. The whole blooming world understands this.

The reason we give them gifts is to help them get a start in life; yet a week after the wedding we expect them to spend a hundred bucks or better on cards and stamps to say Thank You. A hundred bucks that could be better invested in saving for their first home; something that would make us all happy. (Because once they have a home we can all go over and mooch meals off them)

But the real reason I think it is wrong is that the process is reversed. What should happen after a wedding is that the guests should write a Thank You note to the couple. We should say thank you for being brave enough, and in love enough to make a public commitment to each other; a lot of couples seem to lack that courage these days.

We should say Thank You for showing the singles that attend that if they wait Mister or Miss Right will indeed come along; just as it happened for them; and that all the hopes and silent dreams can become real.

And us old folks who have been married for twenty, thirty or forty years should say thank you the most. Thank You for reminding us of the thrills, the excitement, and the spark of love that got us through all these years. Sometimes we seem to get into ruts and forget.

Attending a wedding once or twice every year and hearing the words "For this reason a man shall leave his mother and father, and the two shall be as one:" is better than a weekend marriage encounter.

Kerri, Scott—I thank you.

● ● ● ● ●

Thanks To Experience

I first wrote this piece in Derry, New Hampshire when the temperature was a minus eight degrees out. The sun was bright reflecting off the snow. There was no wind, and every bit of my body and soul was saying it is just too nice of a day to stay inside. Fortunately, thanks to experience I have been taught to reconsider any such urges whenever the mercury drops below ten. Wasn't always the case though and hence, through experience, I have learned.

Uncle Joe called the night before and charged me with driving into Binghamton to pick up bait at a little shop in some guys cellar on a side street down behind the Philadelphia Sales Store on Clinton Street. I was to get four dozen minnows prior to picking him up the next morning. I was a part time singing waiter at Kutch's Restaurant at the time and by the time we cleaned up and I drove home it was two or three in the morning. That didn't dampen Uncle Joe's excitement; "It's cold enough to go ice fishing."

Every year the ritual was the same. He would call; I would panic and go searching for my tip ups; which were always together in my back basket. Really together; five lines and sinkers all wound up in one gigantic mess. I would have to find a file and scrape the rust off the auger so that Uncle Joe wouldn't discover that I had not covered the blade with oil like he suggested at the end of the last season. Every year he would look at the blade nice and sharp; "Yep, putting that oil on really works; a couple of minutes to touch it up and you are ready to go." I always nodded my head. If he only knew that it took me better than an hour to just to find the damn file. And once done I had to try and find my hunting and fishing license which I had hid someplace after deer season. I tend to hide things good.

Getting ready for ice fishing was really a hell of a lot of trauma. I wonder why I did it. It must be a genetic defect passed down through my mother's side of the family. Whatever, as long as there is ice and I can walk—.

We lug all the gear via backpack and banana box a mile into Uncle Joe's secret lake. Concerning the banana box; I should explain that banana boxes were standard ice fishing equipment in my Uncle Joe's house. He had a grocery store and bananas were delivered to him from the wholesalers in metal tubs with high sides. It was Uncle Joe's contention that there was no need to invest in a toboggan as long as he was investing in bananas. So we never did. Few people in Windsor ever understood why the Windsor Market always had sales on bananas each January and February; but I and all my Urda cousins knew.

The snow was up to our knees and the chill factor must have been at least minus thirty. The perspiration that accumulated on our bodies during our struggle to get to the lake served to chill us rapidly once we stopped walking. While I punched holes in the ice Uncle Joe broke off dried hemlock branches near shore and built a rip roaring fire; a fire big enough that just looking at it warmed you. A cup of hot coffee, a pile of snow to shield us from the wind and for a while we were comfortable enough. Occasionally the wind would trip one of our flags and we would get excited about a non-existent fish. We would take turns going to check the holes and scooping the skim ice that formed on top. By the time I checked the last hole the first one would have a half inch of ice on it; it was that cold.

It was Uncle Joe who first noticed the real crisis. When replacing a minnow he discovered that our bait bucket was freezing along with the minnows in it. The obvious solution was to bring the bucket closer to the fire; which we did. Not too close to the fire though; par boiled minnows aren't much better than frozen minnows. The water warmed, and the minnows swam. All was well until we tried to carry a minnow out to the last hole. The poor things froze in our hands. They froze solid before we could get them on the hook. "Need to keep them in warm water out on the lake," said Uncle Joe, and I concurred.

"Go get that rock off of the stone wall." I tried to obey but it was too big, two foot square and five inches think. Uncle Joe came over and gave me a hand; set the stone right in the middle of the fire we did and left it there for fifteen or twenty minutes. After a bit we got a couple of small logs, rolled the stone on the logs and used them to carry the stone out near our tip ups. "You check the holes and I'll get the bucket." The theory was that if we set the bucket on the warm rock the water in the bucket would absorb the heat and thus save our bait.

Somewhere between physics and chemistry I had studied about things expanding in heat and contracting in cold. When I heard the big POP it all came back to me. Uncle Joe set the pail on the hot rock which had been set on the cold ice. He turned around and took about five steps when the rock literally exploded. I'm the only one in the family who has seen a forty pound rock, (now in fifty little pieces,) a minnow pail, two dozen minnows, and my Uncle Joe all air born at the same time. Uncle Joe came sliding across the ice just like Shamu slices across the stage at Sea World; head first and moving.

I ran over to look at the body; figured a piece of rock must have pierced his skull. The body was most appreciative when I got to it; "The hell with me, Go get the minnows."

It turned out pieces of rock had indeed hit him enough to draw a little blood; but Uncle Joe was a fisherman through and through and as such he had his priorities. “The hell with me, go get the minnows.”

Thirty years later my Uncle Joe died, amazingly of natural causes. Father Murphy read a poem for him after the eulogy that went something like this:

May I fish all the days of my life.

May the streams run clear and deep.

And Lord when you catch me in your net

May I be big enough to keep?

MIKE'S ANTIFREEZE

Brother Dick had joined my cousins Evelyn's husband Mike and I on that Saturday and he was in charge of carrying some of Mike's apple cider, Mike's cider that year was of such quality that we cherished it for medicinal purposes. Had it been more abundant and less medicinal nobody in the family would have had to buy antifreeze that year.

In between the Town of Union, where Mike lived, and Little York Lake; in the Town of Willet was an establishment known as the Brown Beaver. Girl friends could be waiting, Mothers could be worried, and wives could be mad; but it was a sacrilege for fishermen to pass the Brown Beaver without at least stopping to use the bathroom.

The Brown Beaver was the only bar I was ever in where after just one beer I saw a horse stroll through between me and the pool table; for real. Everybody in the place just backed up and let it walk through without so much as a blink; twas considered an almost natural thing to the patrons of the Brown Beaver.

Around ten in the morning or there about; the three of us stopped in to pay our respects. We were far from being alone at the bar despite the early hour. Mike starts talking about his apple cider and before long has the bartender's okay to bring in a sample for the morning crowd. Poured each a half glass of cider he did; and a good sample was enjoyed by all. Mike absorbed the compliments so richly deserved and after refills were rendered we three went fishing.

Five-thirty in the afternoon, on our return trip home again we stop at the Brown Beaver to pay our respects and warm up; it had been a cool day.

One of the guys sitting at the bar still had Mike's glass of cider in his hand; hadn't moved in over five hours. Hadn't been for Mike's cider I would have come home early that day.

My cousin Evelyn could have come with us that day. She was certainly invited. "No, No, I'm staying home where it is warm, and comfortable; and I'm going to just relax." She stayed home and her toilet ran over.

When we got back to Union Brother Dick tried his best to explain she would have had a better time if she had come fishing with us; but it was as cool in the Zemberi house as it was on Little York Lake. Dick and I didn't stay for supper.

Communication Gap

The Distance between my Uncles farm to Easter Sullivan's house was about three miles on a road not heavily traveled; perhaps that is why Uncle Fred allowed me to drive his Willy's station wagon when I was about fourteen. It was an easy way to be loved; just be the first person to let me get behind the wheel on a public road.

The generation gap between Uncle Fred and I was not great; maybe thirteen or fourteen years; this morning I was to discover that a generation gap did exist.

I had been driving farm equipment for years and had even driven the Station wagon across the fields and in the driveway a couple of times. Shifting, braking, and the like were not new tasks. Hitting the road and driving up to forty miles an hour for the first time; now that was something else. Uncle Fred provided positive reinforcement.

"You are doing fine." Driving the tractor really helped. You are doing better that I did my first time."

"Okay, you can speed it up a little; now you have it; Good"

"Okay now there is a car coming; get over a little."

"Watch it now; move over a little."

"MOVE OVER"

"MOVE" and with that he grabbed the steering wheel and swerved the car.

And that is when I realized we had a communication gap. I thought he was concerned about the car coming toward us and I kept moving over. Turned out he was more concerned that the mirror on the passenger side was clipping a couple mail boxes as I drove up the road.

● ● ● ● ●

Now I Lay Me Down To Sleep

Uncle Fred communicated very well on the day we used dynamite to blow up the ice jam; Very clear indeed. Just used two words all day long; "No" and "Don't"

A feeder stream into the Gennegenslet Creek had become jammed with ice. Water was now flowing across the flats where corn had been cut last fall. It was trying to find its way back to the main stream and in the process was washing away valuable topsoil and depositing rocks and rubble in its place. Not a desirable situation to be in if you make a living off the land.

The ice jam was extensive and there were huge, irregular cakes of ice two feet thick wedged from shore to shore. Mother Nature had presented a situation that was bigger than any of our farm equipment could handle; "going to have to blow it up."

No, farmers don't know everything; but they do know other farmers who know other farmers who might happen to know. So it was that Bill Hoffman sent us to another old duffer, who, when you looked at, couldn't tell if he had a birthmark on his chin or if the tobacco juice that had drooled down over the years had just permanently stained it. As I recall the floor of his house somewhat resembled a giant spittoon; like his chin it was also spotted and stained. Whatever his surroundings he had experience with dynamite and was willing to give it a try. "Now you got to have a decent flow so when the ice loosens up a bit it will wash away some. I'll take a look at her."

We had found the man alright; but just where do you go to pick up a few sticks of dynamite on a Saturday afternoon in January? Think about that for a minute; if this very moment you wanted to make a little explosion where would you go to get the stuff? For him it was no problem. "Oh, I've got a case or two around here. Might need a hand though; stuff is heavy." I, of course, was anxious to help and immediately volunteered. Uncle Fred immediately said "NO;" then he asked where is it?" The old duffer told him, "right under my bed." And that is right where it was, right under his bed; a whole case of the stuff. My mother and grandmother raised us in a good Christian home with a "when you go to sleep you say your prayers" ethic. I think this guy's mother subscribed more to the big bang theory.

There are four elements required in order to get some punch from dynamite. First is the dynamite itself. The old duffer carried that and we let him get a big head start. Next you need blasting caps. Uncle Fred carried them while mumbling something about me not being able to walk and chew gum at the same time. A battery is required for a spark. Uncle Dave got to carry the battery. Then you need some wire to carry the spark from the battery to the blasting cap. I got to carry the wire, nothing else, but I think Uncle Fred was still worried about me.

The old duffer was a little nervous about the lack of flow as we chopped, dug, and chipped a hole down into the middle of the ice jam; "but. damn, ya don't never know lessun ya try now do ya? And you boys got a problem here now don't ya."

He found him a stick about the same diameter as the blasting cap and sharpened it like a pencil. Using the stick he forced a hole right through the center of a dynamite stick. "Dars'ent use a jackknife; might make a little spark when you don't exactly want er." Next he put the blasting cap in the hole so it formed a cross and then using the wires on the basting cap, weaved them around the cross in a figure eight pattern to secure the cap to the dynamite. Next he taped a couple more sticks of the explosives to the origin one. "We want her to work the first time; too damn hard to dig another hole."

The dynamite bundle was placed in the bottom of the hole and burlap bags were packed around it. Some ice was then packed on top of the burlap. Now all we had were two wires sticking up through the ice. These were twisted to the wires on the spool I had carried and covered up with some electricians tape. Then we went off through the woods; much like the Brits at the Bridge on the river Kwui.

"Everyone get behind a tree and keep your heads down." We did as we were told.

It was a HELL of an explosion. We could hear chunks of ice coming down in the trees a long way from the creek; but most of it came right back down in the creek; there had been no flow under the ice, not even a drop. What a moment before had been big chunks of ice now looked like a load of fresh cement in the creek. That cold cement was blocking the water even more effectively than the chunks. We had accomplished nothing and as a consequence had to pick a lot of rocks off the flats before plowing time. But it sure was one exciting day in January.

Now, fifty five years later, every time I hear someone saying that prayer, "Now I lay me down to sleep," I still think of that old duffer sleeping on top of a case of dynamite.

The Vroman Wedding

My daughter came home from Texas one Christmas with a diamond and a boyfriend. Right away she and her mother started talking about making it a memorable wedding. For the past upteen years we had been invited to at least one wedding a year; some years even more; most I vaguely remember. One, however, try as I might; I can't forget.

David Vroman took Evelyn Urda, my cousin, as his wife, but thanks to my son Brain it didn't come easy. Brian was an alert, vibrant, outgoing four year old. He looked picture perfect as he walked down the aisle holding the pillow on which the wedding band had been placed. I was singing; on the side of the alter, over near the organ; and had a view shared only by Father Hobbs. I was proud of the way people smiled at my little Brian and his cousin Michelle, the flower girl. They were perfect; sweet and perfect. Perfect until he got into the pew.

"Hey, Michelle, look at this." In a voice that could have been heard three blocks away. He turned and pounded the groom's mother on her left breast, trying to point to her corsage. She smiled and the congregation laughed. He didn't need encouragement and immediately responded.

"Michelle, let's do this," in the same earthshaking tone, as he put fingers from both hands inside his mouth and stretched it back to his ears; at the same time standing out in the aisle so that everyone could see.

From my vantage point near the alter I'm trying to desperately to catch his eye and after an agonizing period managed to do so. I should note that this kid could read two years before he entered kindergarten. Long before President Bush said "read my lips," Brian could read the lips of his father. Three times I moved my lips while giving accentuated facial expressions; "SIT DOWN AND BE QUIET, Sit down and BE QUIET: SIT DOWN."

I knew that he knew I was trying to give him a message, because he stood up and shouted;

"WHAT DAD, I CAN'T HEAR YOU,"

Later in the ceremony he grew tired of waiting for someone to take the rings off of the pillow; so he promptly sat down on the first step of the alter. Again the congregation smiled; and his father actually sighed in relief; actually I was hoping he might lay his head down and take a nap.

Mike Hudak

Old Mike Hudak was a friend of my grandfather's, from the old country I think; and every now and then he would drive up from Delaware, pull in the driveway unannounced and be prepared to stay a month or two to "help the boys on the farm." Old, yes, Lazy, not. I don't recall anyone being upset by his visits unless he showed up at a moment when grandma didn't have clean bedding ready. Mike really did help on the farm and made life interesting for me as well.

Once he brought up a cross bow that he had made; could shoot an arrow almost as far and as accurate as the twenty two we kept in the back pantry. Another time he had bent a couple of copper rods and mounted them loosely with staples on a board so that they could swivel. He would then walk around the yard dowsing and accurately found where the water pipes went from the house to the barn. He would walk slowly with the wires pointing in front of him and then as he approached the underground water line the two wires would each swing ninety degrees opposite each other and be parallel to the water lines. He let me try with only minor success. I managed to find puddles in the driveway.

Most of all I enjoyed watching Mike take out his false teeth. Nothing ritualistic about the way he did it. Wasn't a matter of him slipping into the bathroom and letting them soak in a water glass before going to bed; or discreetly removing them in his own room so that folks wouldn't know he had them. Nope, Mike had few inhibitions; he might be laying shingles up on the barn roof and decide that his plate hurt. Would just pop it out and stick them in his shirt pocket. Might be shoveling manure when he got the removal urge and "zip" into his shirt pocket they would go. If he ever got a shirt for Christmas that didn't have a breast pocket I don't think he would even take it out of the box. At age eleven I found it great sport to just sneak around and count how many times he would pop them in the course of a day; got up to five once.

The house in Smithville Flats still stands and deserves a brief description before continuing on. It was a substantial structure two and a half story's high; it had seven large bedrooms. The outside walls were made with three courses of bricks per layer. The layer on the outside looked like a typical brick house; then there was another layer of bricks set perpendicular to the outside layer, and then on the inside was still a third layer of bricks set exactly as the outside layer, Plaster was then applied over the inside layer of bricks. The attic was so big we could have held roller skating parties up there. It had a cellar where the furnace was and then under that was another cellar. When my Uncles bought the place they first thought the lower cellar to be a fruit cellar; later locals told them they could remember back during prohibition when a truck load of furniture left the farm for New York City every week.

There were other stories about how one very wet summer, when everything was nice and green, grass down near the barn was brown and dying. A revenuer by the name of Pussy Foot Johnson drove by and figured it was mash that was killing the grass and he shut the operation down.

Back to Mike and the house.

Mike was near deaf; but what he didn't hear he observed and it didn't take him long to observe that when my Uncle Fred went out on a Saturday night he was prone to taking long Sunday afternoon naps.

When you walked down the hallway upstairs your steps would echo like those sounds in the movies when they march the prisoner from his cell to the electric chair. Thump, thump, thump; the sound would just bounce off the walls.

Deaf old Mike lived in a world of silence; knew how to be silent; and appreciated that everyone did not share his hearing situation.

Sunday afternoon: Uncle Fred is in his bed dead to the world. Here comes old Mike down the hallway, quiet as a church mouse; in his stocking feet; walking close to the walls so the floors wouldn't squeak. Step, wait, step, and wait; took old Mike fifteen minutes to get thirty feet down that hall and into Uncle Fred's room undetected.

He left the door open and then touched off his 30/30 out Uncle Fred's bedroom window. The whole house shook; windows rattled and my grandmother said prayer words in Slovak; least I think they were prayer words.

Uncle Fred was way too young to have fought in the big war; but I bet till this day if you asked him what it sounded like in battle he could give you a pretty accurate description.

● ● ● ● ●

Bird Catchers

Interesting enough my son Brian and I have much in common from our early childhood. The very same kid who made my cousin's wedding so memorable that year also impressed me with his stealth and patience. Between the edge of the lawn and a little diversion ditch I had planted a small garden; so much so that the kids could have the fun of watching things grow as for the food benefits. I did manage to squeeze in four or five rows of sweet corn and by mid August it had grown tall enough that the leaves formed little tunnels that my four year old liked to crawl in. One afternoon I watched as he bent down and then ever so slowly crawled on his hands and knees into one of the tunnels. I leaned on my rake and wondered what the little guy was pretending; what was going on in his mind to make him stop running.

Four or five minutes later my questions were answered; "Daddy, look what I got." There between his hands was a red headed woodpecker with a beak long enough that it alone should have scared him. Brian talked to it; petted it with his thumbs as he held it with his fingers. Then after telling the bird how pretty it was he took it back in the corn and let it go as much to say that "if I want another one I'll go catch it."

The boy has grown into manhood now and there are days when his mind still will go into a thousand directions at once; and yet we often hear him say "come here, fat cat" and the same little boy stops to enjoy the beauty and warmth of another of God's creatures. And his father knows that he grew up just fine.

I too, caught a bird with my bare hands once; and am still amazed that I am alive to talk about it. We had pigeons in the barn and at least once or twice a week my uncles would tell me that if I could just catch a few the family could enjoy stuffed dove; a supposedly great delicacy. They were just there for the picking. "If they are so good why don't you just take the twenty-two and go pick off a few for yourself?" They would respond with something about not being able to shoot because if they missed it would make a hole in the roof.

This conversation had repeated itself throughout the summer and I had thought about it during the winter months when I was often bored in school. By the time school was out next summer I had made up my mind that. By golly, this year I was going to catch a pigeon.

True to form, I hadn't even settled in to the farm routine when I started to hear about "stuffed dove."

There is not a farm boy in all of New York who hasn't known the fun of climbing up into barn rafters and then jumping into a pile of soft hay. That's why we couldn't wait to go to the farm. The rafters in my Uncles barn were high. From the ground to the peak of the roof was better than four stories up., Up near the peak was one small window, One or two panes of glass were missing and it was from here that the pigeons entered and exited the barn.

Climbing up to the rafters and on the big beams was one thing when the lofts were full of hay. Climbing up the walls when the mows were empty was a whole other thing. My Uncles ere working down on the flats and I had some time to spare; it was time. I walked into the barn, sat on a side rail and studied the birds. They would fly in the window and almost always fly to the right and land on one of the four by fours that formed the skeleton of the barn. They would rest for a moment and then fly off to other locations. That window was the only place where I could be sure a pigeon was going to land with any regularity. The only way to the window was to climb the bare walls via the four by four stringers that were spaced every three or four feet up the wall.

I jumped off the rail; walked across the planked floor of the mow and reached up as high as I could and caught the top of one stringer. Found it was rough cut and indeed I could get a good hold. Hauled myself up and before I knew it I was four stringers up and fifteen feet off the floor; which was about one third the way to the window. I got this far and with toes hugging every inch of every board that they could find, and fingers brushing away the chaff on each little ledge I reached for; I went up, and up and up.

The window was now within grasp. My breath was coming out in gasps. I reached up to grab for the window ledge and discovered that broken glass was there and it was slippery. The fingernails on my left had dug into the stringer as though they were pounded in with a hammer. Water was dripping off my nose like a faucet with the tap open. I wasn't a little scared; I was a lot scared. Slowly, oh did I move, slowly, I picked off the loose glass from the ledge and then just as slowly wiggled the jagged fragments out of the window frame, and then after forever, was able to stick my hand outside the window and wrap it around the outside of the barn. Finally I was able to hold something secure.

Spent several minutes catching my breath and with it my confidence. My uncles were still working down on the flats. I could see them and relished in the thought of "I'll show them."

When I ducked down below the window it was only a moment before a pigeon flew right in where it was suppose to; a quick grab and I had him.

Learned a lot about the importance of planning that day.

It had taken every hand, foot, finger and toe to climb that wall; and now I didn't have the faintest idea of how in the heck I was going to climb down while holding a pigeon that didn't want to be held. I do recall thinking that if they could eat pressed duck on Long island; should I fall, they would be able to eat pressed pigeon in Smithville Flats.

Had the pigeon by the legs with my left hand; right hand was back though window hanging on the barn; really holding on and I'm sort of hanging there thirty feet above the bare floor. Pulled up my T-shirt using the hand with the flapping bird in it; shoved the bird inside and managed to tuck the shirt back in my pants. I was now a pregnant eleven year old about to deliver a pigeon from thirty feet up. Success was only momentary; with the big bump in my front I couldn't get very close to the wall to inch my way down. Shoved, forced, and wiggled the pigeon around to my back; bit my lip and started down. Jumped the last ten feet because I just couldn't hold on any longer; never broke a thing.

I'm walking back to the house with my pigeon as my uncles drove up. I hold up the pigeon. They throw their hands in the air congratulating me. I can't hear their voice over the roar of the tractor and think they are signaling me to let it go. So I did.

I know what I told my family that evening; often wondered what the pigeon told his.

False Alarms Maybe

I'm in the middle of my back swing; feet are sliding down the alley. My eyes and mind are riveted on the arrows painted on the boards. At six foot two and weighing ninety six pounds, the only other person in the world as graceful as I on a bowling alley, when in my early twenties, was the comedian/actor Don Knotts. The manger of Ideal Lanes suddenly pages; "We have an emergency call for Don Litchko, an emergency call for Don Litchko. Please come to the counter." I was a manufacturing manager for Robintech at the time and bowled on the company team.

"Don?"

"Yes"

"This is, (name intentionally left blank, as he may still be alive.) The cut off machine is on fire; what should I do." In my heart of hearts as manager of the second shift I would have hoped he would have called the fire department; not that tough of a decision. It was also the first of April.

I told him to "fan it" and hung up.

Went to work the next morning and found the accelerometer cable line down because the cut off machine had burned up. I guess it wasn't a joke.

Stayed at a nationally known Inn in Meriden, Connecticut one night and was awakened by a fire alarm at two in the morning.

Quickly pulled on my pants, and felt the door to see if it was hot. Opened it slowly and when I didn't see any flames or smoke, hightailed it right to the stairway where I met a whole bunch of people walking down from the upper floors. What an assorted mess of half dressed slobs we were; but we had done the right thing and were all safe. By the time we got to the lobby fire trucks had surrounded the hotel. Sirens were wailing; bull horns were bulling and red lights were reflecting off of the snow and windows. Black coats with oxygen tanks strapped on were running through the lobby and still more trucks were coming. The city of Meriden does not take a hotel fire lightly; theirs was an efficient and most appreciated response. Those of us who were safe are standing quiet and waiting for instructions. Nobody wanted to go to their cars if they didn't have to. When bare foot, in a T-shirt and the temperature is only ten above you stay as close to a fire as is safe.

The desk phone rings and the night clerk answers:

"Yes sir we really think it is a fire and not just a drill."

"Yes sir, you probably should get dressed and come down."

"No sir, I don't know exactly where the fire is."

"No sir, I don't think you have the time to pack."

The kid had patience I'll give him that. Had it been me I probably would have told him "No sir, whenever I'm lonely at two in the morning I pull the fire alarm so I can get four hundred people to come down to the lobby to keep me company.

Mr Witt's Wit

Mr. Witt was an eighty year old gentleman who once lived across the street from our sister and brother in law, near Albany, New York. He was a man of small stature who spoke with a heavy German accent; and had an attitude that automatically endured him to everyone he met. Shucks I liked the guy long before I ever met him based on nothing but the stories my brother in law Dave would pass along each time we stopped in for a visit.

"Eighty years old and he is up there putting a new roof on the house. His wife is scared to death."

"Eighty years old and when the wind blew the tree down across the street he was out there with a chain saw before the city crews could even be called; a wonder he didn't cut a leg off."

"Eighty years old and he shovels his drive faster than I can clean mine with a snow blower."

I assumed that Mr. Witt was eighty years old because he remained so active. I was wrong.

When our niece got married she gave me the honor of saying the blessing at the reception. I love all of my nieces and offered words for Leanne and Jeff that may not have been eloquent, but were definitely from the heart. I wanted nothing but the Lords best for these two young people.

After the meal this little man approaches me and says, "Venou talkedupinder itvaslineaenator." I struggled to understand and after a couple repeats came to understand that I was being paid a compliment; "When you talked up there you sounded like a senator." To which I promptly replied, "Oh you mean like Governor Como." And equally as prompt listened in a language quite understandable; "Well not dat good."

Mr Witt was eighty some years old not because he was active; rather because he was a wit.

Wished he had lived on my street.

AIN'T LIFE A

Dirty white sneakers, hairy legs, knock knees, old cutoffs, a pot belly hanging over my belt, and a grey T-Shirt with a colorful San Antonio emblem where the pocket should have been; it was the only T-shirt I had that didn't have a stain on the front. I looked like, felt like, and was, a tourist when I started to walk the streets of Rockport, Massachusetts. Rockport is an artist colony that professes to be the tourist Mecca of all New England.

We were just going to walk around; much to savvy to get caught up in any spending spree. An hour later after conversations like; "wouldn't this be unusual for Christmas?' And, "Don't you just like this?" and "isn't this cute?" the extra fifty bucks we had brought in the morning had dwindled down to less than five; actually much less than five; more like a buck eighty-three; and there were still a couple of items we wanted.

Deep in the folds of my wallet was a hundred dollar bill which had been carried for a couple of years in case of an emergency during my business travels. This was one of my emergencies; if I was to go fishing tomorrow thought it important to go home with a contented wife tonight.

Apparently shop keepers in Rockport had been ripped off by counterfeiters in recent times and when we tried to pay for a three dollar item with a hundred dollar bill they simply declined to make the sale or make change.

On the way back home; many miles inland from Rockport we stopped at an antique/junkshop and I found an item I liked for just a few dollars. I placed the item on the counter along with the hundred and before the shopkeeper could start making excuses I said "Look, I'm sorry but that's the smallest bill I've got." He responded in a slow New England drawl the just dripped with sarcasm the whole length of the counter; all the way to the cash register; "Weeeeell, isn't life a bitch."

I got rid of the hundred. He sold his gadget. And I had ten miles worth of smiles on the way home.

VERMONT DAIRY FARMERS

I am at least semi knowledgeable in the art of dairy farming. Words like Holstein, Jersey, and Guernsey conjure up not only black and white, or soft brown images, with deep blue or brown eyes; but facts like black and white means more milk; brown means more butter fat.

Having, now established my credentials I would like to share my recent observations of Vermont's Dairy farming: the people, the animals and the geography.

Vermont dairy farmers are the most sensitive people in the world. They love their animals as exhibited by a story told to me by a Vermont veterinarian. He, it seems. graduated from Cornell with honors; he was both educated and dedicated. At age twenty-eight he could match diagnosis per diagnosis with doctors twice his age and experience. He had only one problem; any time he went anywhere near a cow it would struggle, twist, turn and belch. The critters would do anything to get away from him. Despite all his training he would have been doomed to failure had it not been for one very sensitive Vermont farmer. "I was walking into the barn when he walked over to me and almost apologetically said; 'Doc, I think the critters would have more confidence in your healing abilities if you didn't walk around the barn carrying a cowhide brief case." That farmer not only saved his animals; he saved a vets career.

Unlike dairy farmers in the rest of the states; Vermont dairy farmers not only classify their animals by breed, they go further and classify them by model. For example he doesn't just own a Holstein; he owns a Holstein SLL or a Holstein SLR. When first exposed to this means of designation I thought they were just acting a bit uppity and trying to mimic sports cars; a luxury no Vermont dairy farmer will ever be able to afford. Upon careful observation it began to make sense when I considered Vermont's geography.

In the whole state of Vermont there are only fifteen flat acres; which are carefully fenced and protected by the Vermont National Guard; fenced because they fear someone will walk across them in mud season and mess up what little they have. The rest of the state is nothing but large hills and small mountains. They didn't call the green mountain boys the "Green Mountain Boys" because they were flatlanders you know.

With this geography in mind, and, considering the years of carful breeding required, one can visualize that:

HOLSTEIN SLR's are cows with short legs on the right side

And

HOLSTEIN SLL's are cows with short legs on the left side.

These models were developed so the animals would be able to stand up straight when walking around the hills. And SLR always walks clockwise around a mountain and an SLL always walks around a mountain counter clockwise.

This is serious business as you can well imagine because once leaving the barn these cows, out of necessity, have to walk all the way around the mountain in order to get back to the barn. That is why those long dairy barns have big sliding doors on each end of the barn. Vermont cows have to go in one end and out the other.

Occasionally an SLL or an SLR decides she doesn't want to walk that far and tries to turn around and come back; this always results in disaster. With the short legs on the downhill side, she becomes top heavy and immediately falls over; rolling three or four thousand feet down the mountain. During that process the utter full of milk gets sloshed, juggled and stirred such that by the time she reaches bottom she has a quarter pound of butter in each faucet and a bag full of butter milk. I have seen the results. Busloads of tourists stop at one of those quant Vermont Country stores. They are offered a free sip of butter milk and butter at fifty cents a pound. All they see is a friendly shopkeeper who is able to eke out a living by keeping the prices right. I walk into the same store and immediately think; "Darn; some farmer around here has had one heck of a bad day; probably had to hire a U-Haul to get that bossy back up the mountain."

It is very important that a Vermont farmer limit his herd to only one model. He can mix breeds, but not models. Here is why. If he only has one model the cows all leave the barn walking in one direction. They play follow the leader, munch a little grass and in general mind their own business. They walk around the mountain; getting back to the barn around five in the afternoon to be milked; just like they are suppose to.

Now then, suppose he has mixed models? The SLL's go out in one direction and the SLR's go out in the other direction. All is well for half a day. Both groups do the follow the leader thing and make pretty good time. Problem is when they get on the back side of the mountain they just don't pass each other and keep on moving. Oh No. When they meet face to face they have to stop and gossip. "I heard little red is going to drop a calf in June; but of course she is keeping it quiet." "Did I tell you where the new hired hand grabbed mc last night?" And they go on and on; wasting hours and hours. You can tell when a farmer has a mixed model herd. If the lights in the barn are on past ten at night and he is still milking; he has a mixed model herd.

Now those who have read me prior know that I always write "clean" articles; most of which would not even require a PG rating. The next paragraph might approach an "R" rating and is included only out of necessity to show the importance of not maintaining a mixed model herd and the seriousness of such.

I overheard this while watching two old gents play checkers near a pot bellied stove in a Vermont general store one Sunday afternoon. It seems that a chap from New York City decided to give up the stress of city life and become a Vermont Dairy farmer. He bought good land by Vermont hill standards; good equipment by anyone's standards; thirty or forty SLL heifers, and one young SLR bull. Two years went by without obtaining a single calf or a drop of milk. Most reluctantly he went to Ernie, one of the afore mentioned checker players, for advice.

Howard, the other checker player, asked, "So what you tell him?"

"Well ya see he asked me last Sunday afternoon, right in front of the wife and young en's and all."

'Ya, I kin imagine; but you had to tell him somethin; so what you tell em?"

"Well I just kinda guided him away from the kids; then I looked him straight in the eye and said straight out, "I think you got an alignment problem."

Now as honest as the answer was you have to realize that was a pretty raw joke for the average Vermont Dairy farmer. It caused such merriment that I don't believe they ever finished the game. One would make a move and the other would say "I think you have an alignment problem; and the whole store would break out in laughter. Went on for hours. The game never ended.

I would like to tell you more about Vermont Dairy farming; but I'm afraid I have shared everything I know.

A Good Man

When the Denisco families get together all are invited, and all are family. There is food and drink, noise, slaps on the back, hugs now and then, and kids running everywhere. Living next door we were always invited and only most reluctantly did we ever say "No."

On one such occasion I was visiting with Grandpa Joe; he was in his late seventies then. A granddaughter walked by with what I think was his VFW cap. Someone asked, "Where did you get that? Joe answered "I gave it to her?"

"Why her. What about the other kids?"

Joe answered factually, "Because she was the one that was interested."

I Looked at him and said "Joe, I didn't know you were in the service."

"I was a bombardier; had to fly twenty-five missions to get back home. The night before my 25th they raised it to 29 because they were running out of trained pilots and bombardiers. But I'm here; I made it okay."

He talked about his plane thinking I was too young to know. I ran home and got a book I had on the history of Boeing. His eyes lit up when we found his "Flying Fortress." I told him how the tail guns were made in Johnson City; at the GE plant where I had served my apprenticeship, and explained about the sand filled concrete bunkers that were used as a firing range when the guns were tested.

He told me what it was like to feel the plane shake; and the noise when those same guns fired; and how he prayed they fired well; "they were all we had."

"Joe; it must have been awful to be told you had to fly four more missions?"

"Well it was, but you know the next one was the best."

I settled in, expecting to hear how he won the war single handed. Instead I met a man.

"Don; on the 26th mission we bombed Holland; I'll never forget it."

"Joe; I didn't know we had to bomb Holland."

"Well the Germans had taken everything; and when you flew over Holland it was very flat. When we looked down, the people, those people in Holland, had taken their sheets and table cloths and laid them in the fields; and they spelled out "THANK YOU YANKS;" with those sheets. Then we bombed them; and he started to tear."

"You see Don, we bombed them with food. Those poor people didn't have anything to eat and we dropped tons of food." Joe choked up and quietly said 'It was my best run." Then he left me and went inside.

I too, choke up; knew that I had just visited with a real man.

Grandpa Joe left us a few years back—

"Fly high Grandpa Joe; Fly High."

Spelunker Training Considered

I live in New Hampshire now and after having experienced several winters and spring thaws am perplexed about taking a spelunker course. In truth I only want to take half a spelunker course; I have no trouble getting into tight situations so see no need to be trained in that aspect; it is getting out of tight situations where I need the help.

I would explore a cave if I found one; but my real need is for pot holes. Here is the situation; the temperatures in New Hampshire keep circulating between single digits and the mid to high thirties. The freeze, thaw, freeze, thaw cycle is tough on our roads. Between our house and the nearest Wall Mart are three pot holes big enough to train astronauts in; big as moon craters and deeper. One neighbor is pretty sure his wife and car are down one of them. Last saw her when she went for groceries and that was four days ago. I asked Eric if he called in to report her missing; said he was considering it but wanted to wait another three or four days; "don't want to get the whole town excited if not absolutely necessary."

Eric is not without compassion and I ask you not to form quick judgments. He just knows his wife; said she has enough hair on her chest to keep her warm; and with a back seat full of groceries she won't starve.

Some of the guys in the neighborhood feel bad about Eric's martial situation. I, for one, do not. The day he responded to that solicitation for mail order brides from northern Maine I told him it was a high risk proposition. He did get one hell of a potato picker though; I'll give him that much.

Sorry, got side tracked for a minute; back to pot holes. Peggy Alterman called the highway supervisor back in December to complain. "Why I could have ruined a tire and knocked the whole car out of alignment!" Peggy knows how to yell; all of her kids left home by the time they were eight, only so much of mom they could take. Al, her deaf husband, still thinks it was his fault because he never listened to them; keeps blaming himself.

The highway super has a patient, understanding manner about him and is use to dealing with the public. In a clam, soothing voice he told Peggy; "Now Mrs. Alderman I know you are upset and I don't mean to add to your unhappiness; but I've got to tell you; if you are having trouble seeing pot holes that big I really question if you should be driving."

Knowing of Peg's lack of success, and not wanting Eric to think I'm an alarmist; I'm going to take a half of a spelunker course, providing I can find one. If I go down, by golly, I'm going to know how to crawl out.

● ● ● ● ●

Wondering In An Old Church

From time to time I have had cause to be alone in an old church. Sometimes I just wanted to be there. Sometimes I was early for a meeting or practice. Sometimes I was way too early, or way to late, having to my dismay forgot which night I was supposed to be there and found myself with plenty of time to wonder.

I have wondered about a lot of things:

I wonder if anyone has ever really seen a church mouse. I never have.

I wonder if God hears the best concert because when the organist comes alone to practice, he or she plays the way they feel and not exactly the way the music is written. I also wonder if when alone if they play a little boggy woggy instead of that church organ music; if I could play I think I probably would—the devil is everywhere.

I wonder how many times a sermon has been given to a thousand ears and only heard by two. I wonder how many times only two were suppose to hear it.

I wonder why; after going to church nearly every Sunday for seventy-one years I can only remember five or six really great sermons (to me); and yet I could recite those five or six to the word to this day. This is a test; what did your priest, minister or rabbi talk about seven weeks back?

I wonder how many people think they are Saints just because they come to church; and I wonder how many people never think about it but really are saints. More, I bet, than any of us critical earthlings are willing to give credit.

I wonder about the workmen who built the church. Did they feel different about going to work each morning when they were building a church? I think I would, even if it were not my church. I would want it to be good.

I wonder why I can be so concerned about persons that I really don't know well; just because I haven't seen them in our old church for a couple of weeks.

I wonder how many folk groups have had the pleasure of having a three year old start clapping, all alone, in the middle of a service just because she liked your song.

I wonder how many people attend a service and still see grandma or grandpa sitting in the third pew; even though they have long left us; just because that is where they always sat and always will.

I wonder about the long wooden beams that support the roof; years old, dry and with long lateral cracks, yet happy to do their job for as long the rest of the building can stand. I have never heard them complain; I like wood and find great pleasure in just looking up at them.

I wonder how many persons have stood on the alter; said "I do," and immediately wondered "What the heck have I just done?" And then thirty years later wondered why they had wondered; because it had worked so well.

I wonder, despite all our technology, why we can't duplicate the smoothness, color, and texture of the wood used for pews;

wood that has had thousands of bottoms slide across it to make room for the late comer.

I wonder how many others, beside me, have had the hell scared out of them while sitting alone in an old church. There was ice on the roof; I turned the heat up because many would be coming to the service in about an hour. When the heat rose it warmed the slate on the steep roof. The ice let go and slid down with a roar. I know instant prayer; and how much dust there is under the third pew on the right hand side of St. Joe's in Salem, N.H.

I wonder how big the pile of money would be if you could stack all that has ever been made at bake sales, bingo games, quilting bees, pancake breakfasts, and chicken-n-biscuit suppers for "our" church. I do know this; when I travel alone and have the opportunity to attend one I do. Better food and much more interesting company.

I wonder, in amazement at all the talent one can find in an old church. Larry can rewire a whole organ without schematics; Chap worked for the railroad but could make the best mitered joints. Cousin-in-law Dave can manage all manner of structure work. Dean could pull a crew together in ten minutes for crisis work parties. Phyllis knows what paint to use to make an aluminum cross gold—it has never had to be repainted in thirty years. Fran Jones knew how to find a man who could bond and laminate those massive hockey sticks that support the cross on top of the church. Frank could knock out a wall and make a kitchen counter inside a week with little or no help. Dad Laga could install a door anyplace when asked. Dorothy and my aunt Mary could make flowers grow in hard pan if they had too. Carm could arrange, rearrange, and then arrange again to make sure the alter was nice. And all of this I saw in one little church in Windsor, NY.

I saw the same happen in Texas when retired Lutheran men and women came in campers from all over the states; and inside of just four months built for a not very rich but growing parish, a new church from the ground up. Today it is a thriving parish in Mansfield, Texas; that church too had talent and has a right to be proud.

And I wonder how many people stop and take a moment to thank God for all the talent living within their own churches.

Now About Aunt Dorothy

When Aunt Dorothy died I wrote a letter to each of the firms with which she did business explaining that she had passed and that the estate would settle any open accounts within a few weeks.

One prominent department store in Binghamton immediately sent me a letter requesting her forwarding address. I, in turn, honestly replied that I didn't know. While I sincerely hoped she went up, and thought she stood a chance, Aunt Dorothy, from moment to moment would do something to cast just a slight element of doubt. For instance:

She came to Mass one Sunday and saw Betty, a dear friend, who had recently been in the hospital. She went over, held Betty's hand, and told her just how good it was to have her back. Through out the whole Mass she had her eyes closed in meditation; you just knew she was praying for Betty. An angel going to heaven; one look and you just knew.

Upon leaving church Father spoke to her, "Dorothy we are having coffee and donuts in the hall this morning. Would you care to join us?"

"Can't. Gotta go home and make old fuzz balls his breakfast." She was going to hell; you knew it. You just knew it.

Aunt Dorothy did not by habit have a foul mouth. To give that impression would be dishonest on my part. She did, however, say exactly what she was thinking; with little concern about who was listening. When she spoke you got the real Aunt Dorothy; no cheap imitation. Aunt Dorothy was four feet high and four feet wide and she learned early in life that a person of her stature had to speak up if she was to be recognized in a group.

Carole came up with the idea that we have a surprise birthday party for her. It was to be a picnic; hot dogs, hamburgers, corn on the cob. It didn't take long to get family and neighbors support. Aunt Dorothy and Uncle George lived just across the way and in winter when all the leaves were off the trees you could see their house from our kitchen.

I had half a sheet of plywood down the cellar upon which I painted "HAPPY BIRTHDAY AUNT DOROTHY." (She was Aunt Dorothy to everyone in town.) The morning of the party, with the aid of a twelve foot extension ladder, I attached this big birthday card half way up a telephone pole where it could be seen by all. And it was; every neighbor that drove by gave us a toot. Everyone saw it except Aunt Dorothy.

Come time for the party friend Gary found an excuse to get her in his car and go for a little ride. As they came around the corner she saw all the people on our lawn, but not the sign, and told Gary, "Look at those bastards; they are having a party and didn't even invite me."

With Aunt Dorothy you never knew.

Occasionally, just for the fun of it, Carole and I would go to Button's Auction House; upriver from Great Bend; somewhere near Red Rock. One night we took Aunt Dorothy with us. She liked old plates, cups and saucers, things of that nature; some of which usually appeared at Mr. Button's weekly auction.

I bid sparingly, trying to pick up a little wine press. Carole won a couple of items. Aunt Dorothy would get in, and out, early. She would mutter a low growling "huuuuph" each time she lost. As the night wore on she had not spent a dime, other than for a hotdog and a coke. I didn't appreciate just how frustrated she was until she started bidding in earnest on the last lot of the evening. Started at 75 cents, went to a dollar, then one fifty; now two—Aunt Dorothy was showing some staying power. Three, now three-fifty; Aunt Dorothy and some old geezer, right there slugging it out. The crowd found it hard to believe; you just don't see this kind of action on the last lot of the evening.

After she finally won with a bid of $4.75; it was I who darn near got a hernia trying to get that four foot long, twelve inch diameter, piece of cast iron drain pipe into our station wagon.

"Aunt Dorothy, do you really want this? What are you going to do with it?"

"Be the last time old fuzz balls will ever tell me I never buy him anything."

I suspect it was. For certain it was the last time I ever took her to an auction.

With Aunt Dorothy you just never knew;—and I miss her.

• • • • •

She Made Me Courious

When you walked into the main entrance of the Alice Freeman Palmer School, now known to most as the old school in Windsor, it was the most predominant feature of the entry. One had to walk up a short flight of stairs to get to the first floor, and, as you climbed there was nothing to look at but Annie's picture.

Annie Flessel lived up past Ernie Brinks saw mill, just off White Birch Lake Road; a beautiful view and excellent location for the artist who for many years was the only art teacher in the Windsor School System.

There are a lot of reasons to remember Miss Flessel. It was she who handed us those blunt nose scissors so we could cut paper tracings of our hands; which we pasted on black paper, which in turn got pinned on the bulletin boards just before parent's night. It was she who taught us primary colors so that we would later understand why when we pee'd into the blue water it would turn green. It was she that always managed to have us make paper candles and holly to put in each little pane of window glass in our school for Christmas. And it was she who students could control if you were smart enough to ask once in each class, "Miss Flessel, when you went to China did you see people with straw hats planting rice?"

I rode a school bus for ten miles, one way, every school day and many a day I would spend the entire trip thinking of a China question to ask Miss Flessel. Once you got her on the subject she would take us on her entire tour. Because of Annie

Flessel by the end of my second grade I knew more about the Great wall of China than I did my ABC's or 1,2,3's. Annie thought she taught art; what she really taught me was the value of curiosity; and she taught me well. She was a stout woman, much like Eleanor Roosevelt, and when she talked she dominated the room; just as her picture dominated the main entrance of the Alice Freeman Palmer School.

The painting was a much enlarged version of a photo taken by a guy named Rosenthal. Every morning as those stairs were climbed I looked up to see six Marines raising a flag on top of a hill on the island of Imo Jima. Annie's picture said so much without words. The men appeared strong, yet tired. The flag was on top and you just knew we had won; our men were the victors. Compared to the battle scars of the ground around the hill the flags colors were bright and beautiful. Because of Annie's picture every person who walked into the Windsor School knew that our town appreciated our military and the men who served. There was no way to walk into the main entrance and not get the message; so good was Annie Flessel's picture.

Being in second grade there was a lot about the picture I didn't know. I didn't know that the hill was named Suribachi and that beneath the men raising that flag, at the very moment they were raising it, there were seven levels of tunnels, rooms, hospitals, conference rooms and block houses all full of Japanese soldiers. I didn't know that the flag in the picture was actually the second American flag raised on Suribachi. The first had been raised minutes before and was then replaced with a larger one so that "every son of a bitch on the island could see it." I didn't know that the flag pole was actually a piece of pipe that the Japanese had used to run water or sewage through the caves inside the mountain.

I thought the flag meant victory. I didn't know that it took another thirty days of fighting before the island was secured. I didn't know that only three of the men in the picture lived to leave the island and eventually returned home. And each morning as I looked up at Annie's picture it never occurred to me that one day I would live within fifteen miles from where one of the men in that picture lived. Rene Gagnon worked in the mills of Manchester, New Hampshire.

But I was curious, thanks to Annie Flessel, and I read and I learned; and have lived a pretty interesting life; because in a big part Miss Flessel shared her adventures; and in the process caused me to become curious.

Mom And Sugar Daddy's

My mother kept an immaculate house; you could eat off the floor and not worry about germs any day of the week. Having raised four of us it was much to her credit that she was able to keep up with the mess we constantly created.

There were times, however, when Brother Richard and I deserved some of the credit for the clean house we lived in. I was reminded of the fact when I went to CVS the other night and paid for a prescription. Under the checkout counter was a monster collection of candy bars. One would have thought that every candy bar in the world should have been there. Upon careful scrutiny I discovered one was missing.

Where have all the "SUGAR DADDY's" gone; those brown sugar, molasses, hard as rock concoctions that came on a piece of quarter inch dowel rod. Those bars that you could suck on and suck on, and, as they warmed up while we sucked, they stretched out to be four inches longer than when we bought them. Then they looked like big brown tongues; and by that time they were sticky; good grief, were they ever sticky.

They were so sweet and so large that no kid could finish one off with one good licking. No way. SUGAR DADDY's were meant to last for a couple of days, at least, and that's where Dick and I helped Mom maintain a clean house. Being young we were prone to just sitting them down when we got tired of them. Might set them down on the couch, the living room floor, top of the bread box, on top of our prayer books; wherever.

Then we would run, jump and play until the sugar high wore off and we needed another fix.

Never once picked up a day old Sugar Daddy without finding a couple of dog hairs or a dead fly on it. Back in those days you could either buy those sticky rolls of fly paper to catch flies, or Sugar Daddy's. I can assure you that both worked nearly as well.

It only took once of taking your dirty Sugar Daddy to Mom to learn she would say "Dirty, you can't eat that;" and she would toss out a perfectly good bar that had two or three days of licking left in it.

Hence forth, no matter what form of crud might have accumulated, or whose mouth it might have been in prior; Dick and I would sneak those suckers into the bathroom, run them under cold water and scrub for all we were worth. I remember one time when I had to use my finger nails to pick off pieces of saw dust when I left one on the chopping block out near the wood pile.

Obviously we both survived and can attest to having not wasted many Sugar Daddy's. And, I think we both deserve some credit for picking up at least some of the dirt we brought into Mom's clean house.

A thought: With the entire so called working mom's in the world today as opposed to home makers; I think there is a need for SUGAR DADDY's to make a strong come back.

The Most Expensive Word

I'm now retired; from what? Well for nearly all of my life I was a foreman, manager, or director of something; much of which I owe to General Electric for giving me a variety of good assignments early in life. And in all that time I formed opinions; opinions not necessarily consistent with standard management practices. What I'm about to share is Litch's version of 20/20; for the benefit of young managers to be; and corporate managers.

The single most costly word in the business world is "BUDGET." (Note I said word and not words; we all know that the most expensive words are "I do."

In all of business, industry, organizations, corporations, institutions and the like there is not another single word that causes so much wasted money as the word "Budget." Every firm spends a zillion man hours preparing one every year.

Then to instill its importance, every manager in the organization is told that their career is dependent upon their performance to budget. (I really think this is an excuse for having spent so much time preparing it.)

At this point all common sense is tossed out the window and there becomes only one GOD. The holy budget; and for its greater good come a whole wrath of bad decisions for the rest of the fiscal year.

Managers no longer cooperate with one another for the good of the company because "It's not in MY budget."

Managers turn away good long term business because of the impact it would have on this year's short term budget.

Managers don't hire needed people to complete projects on time because "I don't have it in my budget."

They delay entering orders because "I have met the orders budget for this month and may need it to look good next month." Then they are surprised six months later when the product is shipped three weeks late or, they have to spend overtime dollars to get it out the door. Of course this is okay because next year they will remember to increase the overtime budget to have enough money to cover it. You may think I'm kidding; I'm not.

They have been known to delay shipments because "I have already met the sales budget for this month and may need it to look good next month. "Then the following week they conduct long meetings to motivate the troops; because our customers expect "On Time" shipments.

I'd bet dollars to donuts that there have been times when our Air Force has been in a position of having planes that cannot fly for lack of repair parts because, "It isn't in the budget." Might not be able to defend the country; might lose a few lives for lack of support; but damn it, we will be able to say we stayed within budget.

Good creative, responsible risk taking managers have been fired because they didn't make a budget. And useless managers who spend their entire careers doing nothing but manipulating the books just to look good, have been promoted because they consistently make their budget.

The bigger the organization the worse it gets. They are so concerned with the budget God that little unit managers actually hire people, disguise them with false titles, to constantly check the books so they can make the budget look good; rather than hiring engineers or marketers that could go out and make the business grow.

You don't have to be in business to verify what I am saying. Watch your town meetings on your public service channels. Every elected official thinks his or her primary function is to micro manage and expose that fifty cents wasted by the previous party; instead of devoting their time to actually solving or improving the towns needs. One county I lived in had a County Farm and some of its surplus goods were sold every year to support it. One official wanted and stiffly asked for an explanation as to why hay sales were down in the month of April; and actually looked a little surprised when told that they had sold all of last year's hay and had to wait for some more to grow. I knew right away he had worked for some firm that would have budgeted sales in order to make the books look good.

One of the most costly budgets is the capital equipment budget because about every November somebody wakes up to the fact that 'We haven't spent all the money in this years budget; and if we don't spend it they won't give us as much next year." So in two short months everyone manages to spend all of the money that they found no need to spend in the previous ten months; most of which never really needed to be spent in the first place.

What bothers me about all of this is that it is such an easy thing to fix. Corporations have had the courage to show that a business can be run in casual dress rather than a suit and tie. What we need now, to really save money, is for someone with the courage to run one business and edict that we will now speak the truth; the word BUDGET will now and forever be replaced with the word "GUESS."

Imagine the difference it would make in the attitudes and lunch room conversations. “Hey Charlie; how you doing on this month’s sales guess? Well to tell you the truth I guessed wrong; but we are going to make a hell of lot more money than I guessed; so I guess it will be alright.”

If we called it a guess; which is all a budget is, an educated guess; good managers would be willing to take reasonable risks; which are what we really want them to do; because the fear factor would be gone.

When we make our planning a God by calling it a budget; everyone gets this false impression that there is something scientific about it; and suddenly a miss requires two hundred meetings and a three hundred page report; all because somebody missed a guess.

One last sharing and I’ll get off this band stand. As a foreman I had an idea that would save the unit a lot of money; but would require a few thousand bucks investment; and my manager said “it is a good idea BUT it’s not in this year budget.” It was a quick return project: we could have saved twenty thousand by the time next year’s budget was approved. I waited a couple weeks; change the wording a little, and called in one of the assemblers who I knew was having some financial difficulties at home; asked her how would she like to have a good idea to turn in for the suggestion program.

She did, and the company paid her well for her good idea; because they had money in the “Suggestion Budget.”

Sometimes you have to help your employer; even when they don’t know how to help themselves.

Maybe Fathers Feel Safer

Use to visit a local fish market that had a large following; their food was fried, fresh and good; and yet there came a time when business just started to drop off.

The last time I journeyed there it took me a good half hour to determine the cause. The girl at the counter had got a pierced upper lip. Where once there might have been a tiny little zit, on occasion; which customers all understood and accepted; was now a big sparkling diamond.

Now it is hard to order fish when you are really wondering:

Why doesn't it fall out?

If it has a clasp on the back side why doesn't her lip bulge out?

It must hurt her gums.

Why did her father let her do it; last week she was a good looking girl?

I can only take a stab at answering the last question. The way I see it this girl has to be extremely careful on dates; because some smoocher with big lips and a good set of teeth could just sort of suck that diamond in, or pop it from its mounting, and go home four or five hundred dollars richer. Why there are probably young men out there that specialize in one date lip diamond snitching. I bet they even act sorry when the girl discovers the diamond is missing and probably even her help search the car for it. Scoundrels, that's what they are; scoundrels.

Yep; her father probably warned her about them; and then figured when it comes to heavy necking—"Not in her life time."

I think fathers who have daughters who wear lip diamonds probably go to sleep feeling safer.

• • • • •

It Took Me A Week

I once bought a young man a doll; true it was a "wrestling buddy;" very masculine, but something about it bothered me. It took me about a week to figure it out.

Driving through the Catskills, on Route 17, near Rosco; looking down at the Beaverkill, one of the best known trout streams in the east. The older gentleman next to me mentioned that he use to camp in this area. I knew him well; my father-in-law; and certainly knew he was not a serious trout fisherman; and the likelihood that he ever owned a fly rod and a pair of waders was slim to none. Further I was surprised when he said he camped; he had never showed an interest in camping. Dad Laga was a quiet man and I just let it pass. A few months later we were sitting alone behind his house one evening and I refreshed his memory about camping in the Catskills and this is how the conversation went:

"Did your Dad take you fishing down there?"

"No, the old man was not much into that kind of fishing; but he was the reason I was there."

"What do you mean?"

"Well whenever things got a little tight on the farm he would load up a load of timbers, or lumber, hitch the horse to the wagon and tell me to go to New York City and sell the whole kit, horse and all. He already had another horse broken in."

“So the two of you would go?”

With a matter of fact tone he said, “No, No, I’d go alone. He would give me a dollar, if he had it and a lunch pail with a couple of sandwiches and tell me to get, and come home with a good pocket full. And I had better do it; because if I didn’t bring home enough I’d really catch it. He would give me hell.”

“Did you have a tent?”

“No, would just sleep under the wagon,”

“How old were you?”

“Oh; twelve or thirteen the first time; probably thirteen or fourteen the others.”

“Did he tell you where to go and how much to charge? He must have had contacts in the city.”

“Nope; told me to get into the city and mind my wits.”

From his father’s farm in Windsor to New York City was better than a hundred and fifty miles through rugged country and few paved roads. With a full load it was a four or five day trip. No map; find your own way; find your own food after the lunch pail was empty, and take care of the horse. Cross the Hudson. A twelve or thirteen year old alone in New York City trying to strike a deal! Once sold he would have four or five days to hike, or hitch rides, back; and all the time constantly worrying if the old man would think he had got enough.

He told me about being afraid that he would get robbed. People traveled slowly; cars were still a luxury and many would camp not having funds for cabins. He would visit others at their campfires because usually they would give a kid some food. He invented stories as to why he was alone; because he didn't want them to know he had money. Gypsies with their fancy cart like wagons were considered common and if he didn't trust them he would wait until after they had bunked down and then "I would walk away in the dark for a couple of miles and crawl up the hill a ways so that they couldn't find me."

A twelve year old alone in true rattlesnake and bear country; only a blanket for cover with no air mattress or sleeping bag; three hundred miles round trip; and less afraid of the dark and wilds than facing his old man and having to say "I let them rob me."

We were having a man's conversation and I believe all he said was true; it just wasn't his nature to tell tall tales. I remember at the time being surprised that he didn't appear bitter about his "old man."

"It was just the way things were; what you had to do; just had to tough it out."

It took me a week to figure out why buying the doll bothered me; then I realized:

Dad Laga never got a doll for his twelfth birthday.

I Want My Grandpa

Bill Howell worked at one end of the plant and I on the other. We might see each other ten times during the course of a year and usually just gave a quick nod or slight wave. Come the first or second Saturday of each December, however, we seemed to form a natural bond that we both looked forward to. Bill was the Santa, and I was Mr. Polaroid, at the plants annual children's Christmas party.

Bill was an excellent Santa, big, soft spoken and gentle. We worked well together. I tried not to flash when he and his young clients were exchanging serious whispers, and, he didn't talk too long when he sensed a kid was only going to sit for five or six seconds. Our success rate was high.

Unfortunately every year there were one or two little ones that wanted no part of Santa. Equally unfortunate, it usually was their parents that wanted the picture the most. We tried our best, but sometimes just had to admit failure.

She took one look at him and screamed; "NO, NO, NO." She buried her head on her mother's shoulder and locked her arms around her neck. For ten minutes we tried. Her Mom wanted her to visit Santa. Santa wanted her to visit Santa. I wanted her to visit Santa; and she kept sobbing, "I want my grandpa."

We got a lot of nice pictures that Saturday; but Santa never got one with his own granddaughter.

Through Different Eyes

While we were out the wood man dumped two cords of fire wood; mostly oak; nice clean stuff in the middle of the driveway.

It is amazing how three people living under the same roof, members of the same family, can see three completely different things in one pile of wood.

Carole saw a problem. "How will we get the car out?"

Lucas saw work. "There goes my day off."

I saw red hot embers between two fire bricks set in the Franklin stove, covered by a grill with steaks beginning to sizzle; on a cold Saturday night in February when the snow is coming down and the wind is loud enough to be heard in the family room. I even saw a crock pot full of baked beans being kept warm on top of the stove; and smelled some fried onions.

Perhaps we have the right combination to succeed in life. If the dreamers didn't dream; if the doubter's didn't see the problems and the workers didn't just do it, not a hell of a lot would get done in this world. We are all needed.

Air Writing

Spent eight hours in a strategic planning meeting and most of it was devoted to what numbers to report on what charts. This was one of those meetings where many got to voice their lengthy opinions; but after the first five minutes it was obvious to me that what the boss wanted the boss was going to get. I admit to devoting a good portion of the day to serious day dreaming. (I try to save my energy for battles worth fighting.)

Got to remember a meeting with Earl Walters early in my career. I was a rookie manufacturing engineer and Earl was the Manager of Manufacturing at the time; he had hundreds of people reporting to him and his position demanded respect.

"Don, what would it cost if we did this instead of this?"

For some dumb reason I had developed a habit of pointing my index finger, pretending it was a piece of chalk, and performing calculations on an imaginary blackboard; probably thought it gave me an air of importance; and besides it gave me an excuse to stall for time until I came up with an answer. Earl was patient and let me calculate the response; even acknowledged that he appreciated my answer. But when I got up to leave he called me back and said "Mr.Litchko, I don't mind you writing on air, but the day you start to erase we both better worry."

It doesn't always take six weeks to break a bad habit.

Earl had a way with words. A few weeks later during a company outing it was he and I as finalists in the bean bag contest. It was midwinter and the American Legion on Jarvis Street baulked at letting us pitch horseshoes on their dance floor; so we tossed bean bags. I was up 20 to 19 and ready to potentially make the winning toss. As I stepped to the line Earl leans over with a smile and tells me "if you make this shot it is going to cost you a $1000.00 come review time." I choked and missed the point. Earl than shot and managed to choke even worse, and somehow he continued to choke until I finally won.

Earl Walters was a darn good man and he taught me an important lesson early in life. Good managers don't always have to win, in order to win.

A Chip Off The Old Block

The Boston Museum of Fine Arts is a monster of a building and after four extended visits I still have not seen it all.

One section contains several large rooms of Egyptian and Roman antiquities. Basically marble bust, after marble bust, with a whole statue tossed in for balance every now and then. Considering how old these pieces are, the tools used, and obvious skill of the various artists there is no question that they deserve to be in a museum. I spent nearly an hour in these rooms, and then, just after leaving, was struck with a thought that caused me to return and walk through the entire section one more time. The result of which is that I can now state with confidence that the Boston Museum of Fine Arts has the largest collection of chipped noses I have ever seen. Nine out of every ten figures has a chipped nose. Some, obviously have been restored; otherwise it might have been nineteen out of twenty that had chipped noses.

I have two theories as to why this is. Theory one has to do with the artist having carved the whole piece; leaving the nose till last; at which time he was tired and when finally hammering that last bit was a little heavy handed. Undoubtedly he said "whoops" or "Oh darn" or something like that when the nose fell off. Having worked four thousand hours to get the piece this far he told the museum "look, I'll give you a deal if you promise not to display it until after I've been dead for three or four hundred years. It is possible the MFA bought many busts in this manner; after all it is an old and well established museum.

This could also be how the carving of heads got their name; every time somebody broke a nose it was a "bust."

Theory number two is much more plausible. Ancient Rome and ancient Egypt was big on the bust business, because there were no Polaroid cameras back then; and from what I have read there were statues everywhere. Now just because there were no BB Guns back then does not mean young scoundrels were without capabilities. They used slingshots and took great pride in trying to knock a bugger off every marble statue they could find. I think this is the more reasonable of my theories. And yes I do know that the carvers did not actually carve buggers on the noses; the pigeons however frequently left good facsimiles.

When considering all of the museums in the world that have marble statuary with busted noses it is also reasonable to assume that the dirt and walkways of the old gardens of Rome and Cairo still contain vast quantities of nose tips.

In Windsor, New York, where I grew up it was not uncommon for folks to occasionally find a flint arrowhead; both my Dad and my Uncles found arrowheads while working in their gardens. My brother Dave has found interesting Indian artifacts while walking the shores of the Susquehanna.

To the best of my knowledge there were no Iroquois or Mohawks in either Egypt or Rome; but I suspect there are still armature archeologists in those places who walk with constant bent heads looking for nose tips; just like we look for arrowheads. And they have conversations like:

"Hey, I found a Hercules last week; put it in the Mason jar along with the Aristotle tip; and that smooth Venus my cousin found."

“Neat, I know a guy who found a Julius once.”

And of course they play the one-up man ship game; “Well that’s nothing, once my grandfather found an Orange Julius.”

Have yet to visit Rome or Egypt but I suspect that once I get to mingle with the everyday folks the conversations will be very much like when visiting with friends in Windsor.

SAVING SOCIAL SECURITY

The argument goes "birth rates are down, so Social Security is surely going to go broke because there won't be enough people paying in to the system to support those who are taking out of it.

Now if that is the case;"that birth rates are so critical to the survival of the Social Security system" then why don't I get more social security money than the people who never had any kids.

Carole and I had four; fed them and a lot of their friends; and clothed them. Spent a fortune on gas driving them all over hells half acre for school events. Had to spend twice as much on furniture and rugs as did a family with no or only one child; they wore out couches and coffee tables faster than green bananas turn yellow. To say nothing of doctor bills, prescriptions and baby sitters; why just the cost of being Santa Claus was enough to send us to the poor house.

And I swear, Scouts Honor, the only reason we had four was to support the Social Security System, and assure that it would remain solvent. I think our contribution deserves recognition. Would seem to me that Social Security distribution should go along these lines:

You had no kids; you get $250.00 a month. You provided no potential providers and you should have been able to save a fortune; even if you were a street sweeper; (who in Boston makes more than most managers.)

You had one kid; you get $500.00 a month. You only procreated enough so that you could pretend you wanted to save the system. (I think these are the people who only put loose coins in the collection baskets at church; you know the type.)

You had two kids; you get $600.00 a month. Why? Come on now you really didn't contribute more than the national average.

You had three kids; you get $1200.00 a month for definitely going above.the call of duty; and the nation should thank you.

You had four kids; you get $2000.00 a month and a free pass to all of the National Parks; because we know that the only way you could afford a vacation was to camp.

More than four kids; You get $3000.00 a month and each check should be accompanied by a personal Thank You from the President. Remember "Don't ask what your country can do for you; but rather what you can do for your country." If you had more than four you did plenty.

Our government would only have to announce once that "your Social Security benefits will be directly proportional to the number of kids you raised;" and every orphanage in the country would be empty inside of two weeks.

Want to send this idea to your Congressman or Senator go ahead. Dave Lutsic had this sign on his desk; "There is no limit to how much good a man can do if he doesn't care who gets the credit." I don't want the credit; I just want $2000.00 a month.

● ● ● ● ●

One Of The Better Funerals

Went to Raymond's funeral, down the Congregational Church, and he was there, up front, laid out in what was a reasonable compromise between what he wanted and what he deserved. Raymond wanted a pine box; his survivors settled on an unstained knotty pine casket. Raymond deserved something better than a box.

There was a little organ recital prior to the service. Most organ players can make reasonable music, but they come in two types; there are note players and those that make you feel the music. This one was a note player; but since Raymond was ninety-one the organist picked songs Raymond might have known as a boy; "On a Hill Far Away," and "I walk through the garden alone when the dew is still on the roses;" and all and all he did okay.

The church was packed and I was surprised when the preacher came out, said a few prayers, and announced that he did not know the man who was sleeping in front of him very well; maybe Raymond wasn't much of a church go-er. I don't really know, but I watched to see if Raymond was going to smile at the situation he put the preacher in; he had that kind of a sense of humor.

I dare say that announcement perked up the congregation a bit. They became rather attentive; listening to see just how young preacher Fred was going to get through this one. I was a bit interested myself. Basically he used information out of the obituary and was then smart enough to call upon anyone who would like to offer a few words. Folks in our town are not bashful.

First up was the president of the K Corporation. At one time the K Lumber company was the largest mill in the United States; turn out that Raymond had worked for them for forty years; predominately out in the woods. “Raymond would come up to me and say “could I see yer for a second.” When he had something to say he never worried about the chain of command and both he and I knew it wasn’t never going to take “just a second.” “But I listened because Raymond had the most logical mind in the whole corporation.”

The President’s son then walked up to the lectern and told how when he was ten his father told the crews to take me out with them and show me how the dynamite worked; and they gave me a hard hat and everything. There was a boulder about half the size of a tracker trailer in the middle of what was to be a logging trail; and by the time I got there it had been drilled, packed and the wire strung. The men all smiled and told me I could push the plunger; but I had to push it hard. I pushed and the second it hit bottom Raymond tackled me and covered me with his own body so that I could hardly breath, Seems the boys had packed er good to put on a show for the bosses son; and it rained granite chips for two solid minutes. Tell you how much I thought of Raymond; I named my son after him.

Another man went up. “When I joined K I was a buyer. I’d look the lot over and buy a stand of timber for the company; and then later Raymond would tell me what I had bought. He knew every tree in these mountains like he was its father. Eventually I listened to him enough that the company started to make money again.” That brought a chuckle.

And another guy told about Raymond and the ground hornets. “The tree had been felled and the trimmers were working on it, when all of a sudden they start running away. "What's matter?' Raymond asked. "Ground hornets, got to go get some gas and torch them out." "Takes to darn long," Raymond told them, and he walks over and starts stomping those hornets to death; brushing them off his pants with his hands; and stomping them. It was some show for a good five minutes; but when he said it was safe to go back to work—it was safe."

So he got this reputation as the hornet stomper and it took him a while to realize that the crews were actually looking for hornet mounds just to see him stomp; and interesting enough it was usually the dozer driver who had the keen eyes for spotting them. Then one day a young buck ran to Raymond and said "Hornets." Raymond grabbed his arm, told him "just you wait a minute." And called for the dozer driver to come over and "shove this tree a bit soo-s we can get at it." And he gave some rather precise directions about where the dozer was to travel. And after that nobody could ever remember Raymond having to stomp hornets again.

For a time Raymond was the village police officer; for all six blocks of the village. One guy remembered reading his nightly report. "I motivated two hobos to leave town early; and later I discovered a couple practicing their "humanity" in a car down behind the railroad station.

I quickly looked around the congregation to see if anyone was blushing; and my instincts told me that Raymond may have caught more than one couple practicing their humanity from time to time; course I could be wrong.

A former Town Moderator told of his regular attendance at town and school board meetings. "Raymond would stand up and say in a deep, deep voice, "Mr. Moderator" and I would know I was in for a long night.

There came a time when the town was being asked for funding to support social issues and Raymond stood up and stated "that while the community should care for those in need he thought the churches should take care of those things, not the town, and besides "I don't think it right that I have to take care of some youngster that I didn't have anything to do with starting." A lady of Raymond's age, across the room, stood up and softly told, "Now Raymond, certainly you can remember that it takes two to tangle." And Raymond reportedly didn't offer much more comment that evening." That too brought a chuckle from the congregation, and I wished I could see in the casket to see if he was blushing.

The moderator went on to tell us that Raymond had once been called to governor's office; so he went; and received a citation for being the best community volunteer and most outstanding citizen in the state.

He was a line Sergeant during WWII, stationed in Maine. He was an outstanding marksman and had the right personality to train city boys how to shoot.

The best story came after the service when a widow neighbor told me, "Don, I walked over to his house Saturday to visit; they had brought him home knowing he wasn't at all good; and he recognized me okay, and had just enough breath to whisper, "I'm sorry, I won't be able to mow your lawn this summer," and then he just closed his eyes.

Everyone loved this Raymond; and I want to be just like him when I'm ninety.

Stoneys

Basically I know of two types of Stoneys in Ouaquaga, New York. One lives in the Susquehanna River and is a favorite bass food. This stoney is a small catfish like creature; two to three inches long. When the fish aren't biting on worms and night crawlers, or if you run out of bait, the savvy fisherman will wade along the shore line, looking for a flat stone that might have enough space under it to house a small fish; then taking a larger rock you "thunk" that flat stone hard. The noise stuns the "stoney" underneath and you can then flip over the stone and catch the little stoney with your bare hand. Unless all the bass in the river are on a diet; the odds are good you will get a bite on a stoney.

I'm not the best stoney catcher; but I'm good enough to pass the techniques on to my grandchildren; and look forward to the day when we can do it.

The other Stoney I knew lived somewhere off one of the side roads in Ouaquaga and he was about the best school bus driver that ever drove the Trim Street—Kent Street route; maybe the very best in the whole Alice Freeman Palmer school district.

Starting down at Route 11; Trim street climbs for better than two miles up to the top of Twitchel Hill, then continues for several more roller coaster miles over to Lester Fours Corners; where by magic it turns into Kent Street. I always thought they should rename the corner "Bush Corners" as that family owned all four corners for as long as I can remember. Kent Street is no less flat than Trim Street. Stoney knew the road well; and every kid on it even better.

He knew about the big bump down below Brinks barn and how to accelerate just enough, at the right time, to hit it and send all the kids in the back seat a foot in the air. He wouldn't do it if we were all acting up and jumping around; but if we were good, and needed a surprise to start our day; Stoney would hit the bump.

Some mornings, as I got on the bus, he would wake me up by saying "good morning" without moving his lips. Stoney was a pretty fair ventriloquist. I remember well hearing "Good Morning Donald" then realizing he didn't say it; lest so I thought, then I'd get to my seat and see him looking back at me in his big overhead mirror, smiling, a little proud that he had pulled it off.

Some bus drivers were yell-ers, "When I tell you to sit; I mean SIT." There were periods in my young life when seat switching seemed to consume a lot of the ten mile ride home from school and I got to know the yell-ers close up like. Although I knew I had it coming I didn't like the yellers very much.

Stoney was smarter than the yellers. I had caused him some serious concern, bouncing from seat to seat one night; next morning when I got on the bus he told me to sit right behind him ; in the first seat. Even though he had asked me nice like I was pretty certain I was being punished. He didn't say much while he picked up the Doolittle, Shiel and Gleason kids, but then when he had some open road he leaned back and told me he needed some help; "Should we ever have an accident I need someone I can trust to bring the Emergency Kit off the bus and wonder if you would mind being my right hand helper?" Course the emergency Kit was located right next to the driver's seat, up front, where he could keep an eye on me.

Talk about suddenly feeling important, holy cow, my chest puffed out; I went to the library to get a first aid book; and studied it with a passion. A couple of days later he squealed the brakes, pulled off the road, and yelled "Accident drill—Everybody out;" and that tin emergency kit was outside, along Stoney in a flash. He told me I did "great."

A good portion of my career was spent in positions where I had to motivate people; took classes, attended management seminars; and yet never learned a more important lesson than when I realized the difference between Stoney and the "yell-ers."

There were two kinds of Stoneys in Ouaquaga, New York; and I have been fortunate enough to know both.

Awards Not Awarded

Come the end of each school year when those of us just happy that our kids, nieces, nephews, and grandchildren will graduate; we have to sit through a couple of hours of listening to some high school dignitary hand out awards for English, Area Studies, Biology, Science, Music, Art, Perfect Attendance, and then introduce the class Valedictorian and Salutatorian.

I have no problem with recognizing and applauding these achievements and achievers; but do have problem with the important traits and talents that are not recognized at most high school graduations.

My hang up is that most of the awards are based on good memories and a lot of discipline. "I studied, I did my homework, I did exactly what was required; therefore I achieved. Unfortunately that is only half the equation to living a successful and productive life.

There are a whole bunch of other attributes required for success; that our high schools fail to recognize. Here are some of the awards I'd like to see presented at every high school graduation:

THE BEST QUESTION ASKER AWARD—Students ought to be awarded for asking good questions; the most thought provoking; the ones that stump the teachers; the ones that make everyone else in the class stop and think. Marlowe and I have been good friends for years, fish together, worked together, have a lot in common; but high on my list of why I enjoy his company are his questions. His "I wonder whys" and "what do you think abouts" make for great conversation and often drive me to thoughts I wouldn't otherwise have even considered. Good question askers are more than just important, they are critical to a good life; and they should be recognized.

THE BEST PRACTICL JOKE AWARD—Practical jokes should be encouraged and recognized. I'm serious; a good practical joke requires creativeness, vision, an awareness of your surroundings, planning, execution and courage; every attribute we want in a good manager or leader. Yet for some reason our schools put down the practical joker as one who is acting childish. It is time to recognize talent when we see it and applaud the practical joker. To this day I still want to know how the big bull on the roof of the Vestal Steak House, which was located on the busiest highway in the Triple Cities, got stolen and later returned with no convictions.

THE BLIND AWARD—There ought to be an award for the student who goes through four years of high school completely blind not only to the color of his or her classmates, but to all of the clicks, the snobs, the over achievers and non-achievers, and is able to deal with each classmate on their individual merits alone; and not based on what society has preprogrammed them to think. There are students like that and they should be recognized as the ones who will build better communities. We need more truly blind students in this world.

THE "AT EASE" AWARD—There are students that it matters not what the crisis, the situation, the predicament they walk into, can just make everyone comfortable, they can bring a smile, share a care, listen, and they can diffuse; they have a knack for just putting everyone around them "at ease." Lord, how we need more people like them. We ought to recognize the "AT EASIERS" we have, as being examples for the rest of us.

THE CRAFTSMAN AWARD—There ought to be an award for the student who can best work with his or her hands. I believe we underestimate the ability of teenagers to produce quality crafts. Fine Woodworking magazine once told of a high school in Pennsylvania that featured the best piece of furniture produced by a senior, right on stage, during graduation. Windsor chairs, exquisite Chippendale dressers; hand cut dove tails so fine you can't see the cut line; all of heirloom quality. There should be a craftsman award and a craftsman scholarship. Most scholarships are given to students who are going to attend college; why not scholarships for craft schools. Pride of workmanship is worth our investing in.

THE COMMUNITY LEADER AWARD—We should make this the most coveted award of all; so that students will understand what a community leader really is, prior to graduating and having the right to vote. This award should not go to the sport hero, the best looking cheerleader, or the class president who won the popularity contest because of personality, smiles and nice guy image. It should go to the student who best volunteers for community betterment outside the school, or the one who attends a town board meeting and has the courage to stand up and try to make a difference; or to the one who saw a community need and rather that making a big deal out of it by complaining; just went out and fixed it. There are those kinds of teenagers in every high school and they should get the coveted Community Leader Award.

I have read at least a couple thousand resumes in my lifetime and oh, how I would have liked to have read, just once, about someone who had received one of these awards. I would have granted them an interview just for the joy of meeting them.

MIRACLES

Not often that I'm asked if I believe in miracles; but admit right now that indeed I do. I also believe that few people appreciate a good miracle when they see one; take for instance a church breakfast.

Every church breakfast starts with a simple good intention; ends with satisfied and pleased patrons; and if intended to be a money maker, always ends with an improved pocketbook. The miracles of miracles occur with all of the interaction that takes place in between.

Start with the planners and unplanners. A few people get together to plan the operation even though a few hundred were invited to participate. Somehow all of the people who didn't have time to help plan and pre-volunteer show up in the kitchen on the morning of the breakfast ready to help—it's a miracle.

Some are humble and just ask "tell me what to do;" they are few in number and definitely are walking miracles.

Some. the not so silent majority, are opinionated and that is when the real miracles start. "That's not the way we use to do it." (*Yes dear, but now we cook with gas, not wood.*) 'Do you really think they will like eggs THAT way?" "The recipe I always use is."

Every church breakfast serves scrambled eggs. Why? Because they sound so simple, so easy. Oh yeah—try these variations—and if you haven't heard of them before it is obvious that you have never worked at a church or community breakfast. You need to get up and volunteer some morning. No wonder you don't believe in miracles.

"I just scramble the eggs."

"I always save some beacon grease and add a little salt and pepper."

"The way I do it is salt, pepper, the eggs of course, and a little milk."

"That's good, but shouldn't you add a little baking powder to fluff them up?"

"Cheese; they taste bland if you don't put in some cheese."

"Well, what I do is dice up some peppers and a little onion to make them look nice."

And I'm here to tell you that when a couple hundred people get fed the incredible, eatable egg after all that bickering; "IT IS A MIRACLE."

And this is just the start; there are at least a dozen more miracles that take place at a church breakfast.

There is the "how big do we cut the potatoes for home fires "miracle."

"The serve the pancake syrup warm or cold "miracle."

The "Why didn't you get the food donated so we could make more money" miracle; as always asked by a person who never attended a planning meeting in her life, let alone would have the courage to go to her grocer and ask for a donation; but YOU should have done it.

The "we should use paper plates and not have to wash all those dishes" miracle."

And then, even though every seat in the house is filled and you are running out of food, there is still the "You should have advertized more" miracle.

I have never seen a sinner kill somebody in the kitchen at a church breakfast; I think that's a miracle. (A sin being any bad thought, word or deed; and I know that there are those that have done a lot of bad, bad thinking, and some quality mumbling; while cooking for a church breakfast. They might have done the deed, if only they had a gun.)

I have never heard someone complain about having attended a church breakfast and that is at least a minor miracle.

And I have never seen a kitchen crew go home dead tired; without still feeling good that they were part of it. And that is the biggest miracle of all.

Show me a man who has never seen a miracle and I'll show you a man who has never worked a church breakfast.

SHE REACHED THE TOP

On my list she is, without question, one of the top ten; and her biggest gift to me was demonstrating that senior years can be you're most exciting, most fulfilling, most productive. Between Jewell Farrar and the movie Grumpy Old Men I entered retirement with a definite jest that would not have developed otherwise.

It was Jewell that made a special trip; to our house once just to encourage me to write; and her "You just have to do it, because you can make people remember, and smile, and that's important," was spoken with so much sincerity that I have never wrote a piece without a little bit of Jewell whispering in the back of my brain.

It was the retired Jewel that joined the Peace Core and wrote a wonderful journal telling in part what it was like to be black and suddenly live in a place where blacks were the majority and not the minority. And through her sharing my eyes and mind were opened just a bit more.

In the journal she told of families that accused her of lying to their kids; Jewel was a teacher. Surprised at the accusation she asked "When did I ever lie to your children?"

"You are teaching them that man has been on the moon and you know that isn't so." And better than any National Geographic feature Jewell taught me that not all of the world watches TV; or for that matter even cares if there is a NASA or not.

I watch the Antique Road Show and often wonder how anyone could be so impassioned with a piece of cracked pottery that with a single glance they can tell where it was made, by whom, painted with exotic glaze number such and such, on the 15th of December in 1827; enough so that I sometimes wonder if I am okay. My mind wants to know a little bit about everything; not everything about one thing. My thoughts sometime jump around from day to day; and then hop back to where they were a month ago.

Then I met jewel; and felt okay.

I only knew Jewel in her senior years; and here is a sampling of what she did in that time:

Set up a remote family, fly in, camping trip to Alaska. One week with no other human contact; no phone, no power, no bath or shower; whatever happened you were on your own. And Grandma Farrar jumped off into a glacial lake; perhaps in her birthday suit, because "Come a couple of days without a bath or shower you can smell a little ripe."

She may have eaten dog while on at trip to Ecuador; while satisfying her desire to see a live volcano.

Celestial navigation; Jewel could sail by the stars and practiced in the Long Island sound.

Care—about everybody; she was a long time child advocate in some real Connecticut Courts. She worried about, and loved, kids; all kids.

I once invited her to come to New Hampshire and see the sled dog races in Laconia. She did better; signed up with Elder hostel and took a week long sled dog course. I have watched sled dog races; Jewell drove a team and rode the sleds.

Scuba diving; she took the course just for the experience.

Read; Marlowe told me that when growing up in his house a trip to the library was a weekly thing; and three books a week was the expected reading; and through Marlowe she gave me, without question, the best read friend I ever had. "And she practiced what she preached."

I have taken dozens of people to the top of Mount Washington; some were impressed, some nervous, some excited, but never was one as thrilled as Jewell; head out the window looking over the edge (there are no guard rails on the Mount Washington Road) sometimes her nose was pressed against the windshield, looking up trying see it all; afraid she was going to miss something; and her mind was working so fast generating "I wonder why" questions that she almost couldn't get them out. She was having such a great time that when we got back to the bottom I was tempted to turn around and drive back up; just to watch her facial expressions. She made my day.

"And when I was born he looked at me and said "now isn't she a little jewel;" and I was named Jewell from that day on." I never met that prophet in Marlowe's family, but to be certain he was; because indeed Jewell was a jewel; and she sparkled every time I was with her.

Then came a Saturday when Jewel was scheduled to take a bus trip adventure with some friends; and when she didn't show up on time they found that Jewel had decided to take an even greater adventure.

Just like her to want to try it all.

Almost Forty-Five Years

In a couple of months we will start our forty-fifth year together; and after forty-four years she knows;

That I am a morning person; and I know she walks early, but doesn't really wake up until after lunch.

That I rub my feet and toes while watching TV in the living room; and I know she does the same in the privacy of the bathroom; she has told me more than once.

That I like to be early for everything; and she thinks there is not a place on earth that I can't drive to in five minutes or less after she gets in the car. She has such faith; I have such ulcers.

That she can take a near empty refrigerator and make a five course meal for ten with no problem; and to do the same I would have had to plan three days ahead.

That I can get a thought in my head and sit writing with a passion, until late hours; and I know what it is like to wake and find her missing from bed; only to hear the buzz of her sewing machine at three in the morning, because, "I want the girls to have this for Easter." And I know I will be prouder than the dickens of what she makes.

That she gives me time to work alone in my shop; and that I give her time alone to paint.

That if I say "I can do that." She has never said no, and has always been my best cheerleader.

Forty years of rheumatoid and if I ask "hurting today" I know the answer will always be the same "just give me some time and I'll be okay." Never do I hear a complaint more than that.

Neither of us can walk by a baby without wanting to touch its toes.

My anxieties are always countered by her patience.

She has stacks of cloth in her sewing room that she will find a use for someday; I have stacks of wood that I know I will use someday. Neither of us know for what.

We get as much pleasure watching birds and bears in our back yard as we do attending a good concert; and thoroughly enjoy both.

I walk through a whole museum licitly split to see what they have and then come back to the parts that interest me. She reads every word of every sign, starting right at the entrance, and feels cheated if rushed; and then, on the way home, we fill each other in on what the other has missed.

We have literally built homes with our own hands from the ground up; raised four great kids, a dog, a few cats, a guinea pig or two, and tens of thousands of honey bees; maybe that's why we have eight sweet grandchildren. Had some darn tough years and some darn good years. We take pride that friends can walk in our door, take their shoes off and relax; and have been blessed with ever so many good ones.

We exchanged our vows in the old, now gone, St. Mary's church in Kirkwood. It has been an interesting run.

Will the marriage last? There is parrot sitting behind me that has tested this marriage beyond all possible comprehension; and we are still together. (I have told her that if she goes first the parrot is going fifteen minutes later.)

And the best part of all these years together, with all our differences and all our "alike's;" I still love her and know that she still loves me.

Thankful For Kathleen

Kathleen; I know when Kathleen walks into the church; long before I can see her because she shouts "HI" to the first person she sees. Sometimes she catches sight of the Deacon and in a very, very loud voice tells her mother, "Same guy as last week."

Often I have seen her mom lean over and whisper words like "Okay now, we are in church and you need to be quiet." And Kathleen responds by shouting "OKAY I WILL" with so much enthusiasm that she rocks the whole church. Our church holds six to seven hundred persons easy.

Her noise might disturb some "purist prayer people" who like to kneel before Mass and have a silent moment with God; but not me. I'll tell you why.

There comes a time in every Mass when we offer the Lord's Prayer. Sometimes Father leads the congregation in the recitation; sometime when I cantor we sing the "Our Father."

From my vantage point on the alter the view of the congregation is very open; I can see them all. Most sing with me; some sort of mouth the words, and a few just watch me; maybe to see if I am going to hit a bad note or miss a word; but no one does what Kathleen does; Kathleen cries. In that whole church nobody feels the power and the beauty of the words like Kathleen.

In that whole church nobody else is open enough to let their feelings show.

Nobody but Kathleen cries.

Kathleen was born with Down's syndrome; and I am so happy to know her.

An Inquisition

Niece Catherine, whom I love dearly, announced her engagement to Dom; a step taken without first consulting her Uncle Don. Wanting to trust her judgment I still find myself full of questions that only an Uncle can ask; I, after all, want this to be a lasting marriage. Having survived years and years of bliss myself I had hoped she would consult "the expert." I offered this check list while she still had the diamond, but not yet recited the vows. There was time to reconsider; if necessary.

A father might wonder if this potential groom has the where with all to support his daughter; an Uncle wonders if he has the where with all to support the entire family. I like to think big and to date not one of my own, nor has any other niece or nephew married into money. Catharine, you are my last hope. If I'm going to spend the rest of my days sitting in a rocker, on the front porch, sipping mint juleps; it is up to you.

Does he like beer? Not critical, but relatively important. I don't recommend you marry a boozer; but there will be times when the bills are high and the pay check low; the kids are loud and the in-laws intrusive; the dog will poop on the living room rug; you will be feeling out of sorts, and the sink won't drain; all on the same day; and having a husband that says to himself "this calls for a beer;" as opposed to one who declares "I don't deserve all this" and then skips town, will be a great comfort to you.

When he shaves does he rinse out the sink or does he leave those little black, lice like, looking things in the bowl; anchored there with some dried out shaving cream? Remember, when you get him you get his whiskers; on or off him.

And what about ear wax? This will be important in your older years. Does he just use a Q-tip and discard; which you may find acceptable at this point of your life? But I ask; will he be able to clean his ears with the tip of the bows on his glasses when he is sixty; and then pat them into his hair in order to keep those glasses from falling off his nose? May not seem important today; but there will come a time. You have no idea how much time is wasted each week when the two blind seniors in our house can't find their glasses. Don't marry a man who is squeamish about the use of ear wax.

Is he spontaneous? Will he wake up some morning and just say "Oh the hell with it; let's go to Canada for breakfast;" and then do it. Many a morning your Aunt Carole tells me, "Can't you just sit still;" but she never says "no." And ten minutes out the drive, usually less, the smiles start and we both have some dandy times. Make sure he is a bit spontaneous; it will be good for both of you.

Does he dream? Husbands without dreams have nothing important to share. When he shares dreams you get to really know him; and when you share your dreams he gets to know you. Make certain that there are going to be two "dreamers" in this marriage.

How about Thanksgiving? When the guys have had a couple of beers while watching football and then the turkey is put on the table; will he be man enough to stop all the chatter and say "let's say grace;" and then choose words that will make everyone feel like family; and let God know that way down deep he cares. How will he be at Thanksgiving?

Does hc giggle? Will save you a bundle if he does. Proven fact that people who smile, laugh and giggle, often are in general in better health. With the price of health care these days marrying a giggler just might make good financial sense.

Notice dear Catharine that I haven't asked if he loves you. I have no doubt; what's not to love when he can get you, and an Uncle like me tossed in the same bargain; just how lucky can he get.

* * * * *

Wine At The City Line

Once upon a time there was a bar type restaurant across the street from the former GE plant in Johnson City, New York call the "City Line." No two hamburgers ever looked alike because the meat was placed on the counter; pounded to the proper thickness with a sledge hammer and then sizzled to death on a grill; the degree of doneness being determined by how many people were yelling for beer at the bar. Beer sales always took precedence; and many a hamburger was either very well done or hardly done.

Tommy, the owner, was bigger than stout and quick with words; "If you don't know what you want move out and make space for people with real money." "Is this what you ordered? "No." "Well eat it anyway I don't have time to make it pretty." "You owe me a buck and a quarter; put it up; who's next?" And we would laugh at him and we would eat.

This was a beer joint in the truest sense of the words. Tommy was there to sell beer.

In my working youth I frequented such places from time to time. Had this friend, Jimmy Wit, a Polish lad, who also frequented Tommy's place and who one day asked Tommy for a glass of wine.

Tommy looked at him queer like and said "You want what?"

Jimmy Wit responded; "A glass of wine damn it; it's about time you catered to a higher clientele; and I'm it."

From somewhere Tommy found a glass of wine; muttering the whole time about "how can a man make a living selling men "sissy girl drinks."

This offends Jimmy Wit such that he left the place, only to hang out by the front door; where he convinced all the regulars as they left, "tomorrow everybody order wine." And come tomorrow we did.

Tommy runs out of wine in two minutes. Wants to know; "What the hell is going on?" "Where is that Witkowski; curse the day I ever let him in here." Jimmy Wit loves every minute of it. An angry Tommy wants to know. "Do you guys want beer or not?' And all the regulars yell "Not" and walk out. For some it was a hard walk; maybe the first time in their lives they went through a lunch without a beer.

Next day everybody goes back to the City Line; twelve bottles of wine had found a home behind the bar. And they remained behind that bar for the next twelve years. Jimmy Wit just couldn't get folks to order wine two days in a row.

Every now and then someone would start to feel bad about how we made Tommy waste all that money; I would look behind the bar and realize that the best wine in the place was labeled Muscatel; and there were bottles labeled vintage "June;" and I for one never lost a night's sleep over the matter.

Now Why This Book

I always write so that I won't be ashamed if one of my grandchildren reads it. Not a bad rule to be incorporated by all authors.

Mostly I write for my grandchildren; I want them to know that their grandpa tried lots of things, was not afraid to take chances, make mistakes, and most of all had the ability to laugh at himself; all traits that have served me well; all traits I hope they inherit.

Once read a phrase "My desire is to inspire before I expire." I hope that you, the reader, will take the time to realize that your life has been even more interesting than mine and then take the time to write your own stories. Don't worry about your ability to spell, your knowledge of punctuation, and all the rules taught us in grade school. Write just the way you talk; if when you read your paragraphs they sound like you talking—you did it right.

Too many wonderful stories have been lost because people think "I can't." You can and I'd love to read it. TRY; there will come a day when your grandchildren, nieces and nephews, will love you for it.

Love you all
From a hill far away
In Conway, New Hampshire
Where sometimes even the owls don't give a hoot
Litch aka Dad aka Uncle Don aka Cuz aka Grandpa